First published in Australia, 2025

by Speculative Insight

www.speculativeinsight.com

Cover © Jessie Marshall

Layout by Alexandra Pierce

All rights reserved.

No part of this book may be reproduced in any form or by any electronic or mechanical means, including information storage and retrieval systems, without written permission from the author, except for the use of brief quotations in a book review.

ISBN: 978-1-7643660-3-8

"Families of the Future" copyright © 2024 by Nina Niskanen

"Romantic Lead Balloons: anti-romance and masculinity in the Discworld" copyright © 2025 by Tansy Rayner Roberts

"The SEA is Whose?: Ethnic Entanglements in Southeast Asian SFF" copyright © 2025 by Ng Yi-Sheng

"Untangling Quiet" copyright © 2024 by E.D.E Bell

"Celibacy & the Single Wizzard" copyright © 2025 by Tansy Rayner Roberts

"Forensics for Fairytales: magic or science in speculative detective fiction" copyright © 2025 by VJ Knipe

"What Lies and Threats: History and Nationalist Myth-Making in *The Lord of the Rings*" copyright © 2025 by Abby Roberts

"Reimagining Disability in YA Fantasy: Exploring Harper and Rhen in *A Curse So Dark and Lonely*" copyright © 2025 by Emilie Morscheck

"In the Grim Darkness Of The Far Future There Are Only Warriors" copyright © 2025 by Kyle Tam

"Men Who Respect Witches IV: Kings, Manhood and Morris Dancing" copyright © 2025 by Tansy Rayner Roberts

"The Dublin Portal... Or The Dublin Intrusion?" copyright © 2025 by Val Nolan

"Should Galadriel have taken the Ring?" copyright © 2025 by Nick Hubble

"Fox Girl: A Speculative Journey" copyright ©2025 Lee Murray

CONTENTS

Introduction	v
1. FAMILIES OF THE FUTURE Nina Niskanen	1
2. ROMANTIC LEAD BALLOONS *Anti-romance and masculinity in the Discworld* Tansy Rayner Roberts	12
3. THE SEA IS WHOSE? *Ethnic Entanglements in Southeast Asian SFF* Ng Yi-Sheng	22
4. UNTANGLING QUIET E.D.E. Bell	34
5. CELIBACY & THE SINGLE WIZZARD Tansy Rayner Roberts	45
6. FORENSICS FOR FAIRYTALES *Magic or science in speculative detective fiction* VJ Knipe	59
7. WHAT LIES AND THREATS *History and Nationalist Myth-Making in The Lord of the Rings* Abby Roberts	74
8. REIMAGINING DISABILITY IN YA FANTASY *Exploring Harper and Rhen in A Curse So Dark and Lonely* Emilie Morscheck	89
9. IN THE GRIM DARKNESS OF THE FAR FUTURE... *There are only Warriors* Kyle Tam	104

10. MEN WHO RESPECT WITCHES IV　　　115
Kings, Manhood and Morris Dancing
Tansy Rayner Roberts

11. THE DUBLIN PORTAL...　　　129
Or The Dublin Intrusion?
Val Nolan

12. SHOULD GALADRIEL HAVE TAKEN THE RING?　　　143
Nick Hubble

13. FOX GIRL　　　157
A Speculative Journey
Lee Murray

Subscribe　　　181

INTRODUCTION

Speculative Insight is now in its second year of publication, and I remain delighted by the authors who have entrusted their words to me. Several of the authors in this collection are people who saw our very first open call for pitches and responded - with great enthusiasm - to the idea of writing an essay for this relatively new venue. With essays covering everything from disability in YA fantasy to heroes in Warhammer 40k novels, what we mean by "quiet fiction" and whether Galadriel should have taken the ring, there's a fantastic range of topics. There are some familiar names from 2024: Tansy Rayner Roberts, continuing her "Pratchett's Men" column; Nina Niskanen, who last year wrote about cargo ships in space, here looking at families of the future; and Lee Murray, contributing the bonus essay in this collection, an examination of her journey as a speculative fiction author through the myth of the fox spirit.

It was a great honour earlier this year when the January-December 2024 collection of *Speculative Insight* essays was awarded the Convenor's Award for Excellence at the Aurealis Awards, Australia's juried awards for fantasy, science fiction, and horror. The Convenor's Award recognises work that doesn't fit into the written (or graphic) fiction categories. To be recognised in this way in our first year of publication was tremendous.

Thank you for reading: the journal could not exist without your continuing support. Remember to tell your friends!

Alexandra Pierce

Ballarat, Australia

June 2025

About the artist:

Jessie Marshall is an art student from Melbourne, living and studying in Vienna for now. The artwork featured on the cover is an original piece of embroidery, called "I looked and looked." You can find examples of her work at www.instagram.com/jessiejoymarshall/.

1

FAMILIES OF THE FUTURE

NINA NISKANEN

At the 2023 Eurocon, in the summer heat of Sweden, I joined some really smart folks on a panel about families of the future. When Alex was putting together the line up of writers for the first year of this journal, she asked me if I wanted to elaborate on the topic in a written format. And yes, I absolutely did because it feels like all the fiction that I write somehow always comes back to that; family and all the forms that it takes. Even if it's not central to what I write, to me, fundamentally what makes us human is the other people around us. And part of that is also who we choose to keep around us and who we want to call family.

In this essay I want to explore family in science fiction through the lenses of Octavia Butler, Charlie Jane Anders, Starhawk, John Scalzi, and Martha Wells. Be forewarned that there are spoilers for the following books: the Xenogenesis series by Octavia Butler, *Victories Greater Than Death* by Charlie Jane Anders, *The Fifth Sacred Thing* by Starhawk, The Old Man's War series by John Scalzi (specifically, *Old Man's War, The Ghost Brigades, The Sagan*

Diary, *The Last Colony*, and *Zoe's Tale*), and the Murderbot series by Martha Wells. These books all have a very different view as to what family means and also, in some ways, a really similar one.

Scalzi's Old Man's War series presents a somewhat conventional view of a family; a man, a woman, and their offspring. Said offspring is adopted from a dead man, and the woman is the clone of the man's dead first wife, but it still looks very much like what is currently thought of as a conventional family. All that's missing is the second child and a golden retriever.

Octavia Butler and Starhawk, on the other hand, explore what families might look like with multiple adults and their offspring. In Butler's Xenogenesis, families always consist of two humans (female and male), and three Oankali aliens – a female, a male, and an ooloi, a third gender and necessary part of the Oankali reproductive cycle, which the humans are also forced into. Starhawk, on the other hand, abandons all structures, and imagines an interesting utopian/dystopian future where in some places, the people live mostly in happy, hippy polycules[1] of their own choosing, and some places are still dealing with authoritarian nightmares and the associated forced monogamy.

Lest we forget the found families, we have Charlie Jane Anders, whose *Victories Greater Than Death* sees a group of human teenagers recruited onto an alien spaceship, where they promptly band together against some terrifying villains and become family for each other, having abandoned the families they've left behind on Earth. And last, but definitely not least, Martha Wells' Murderbot series follows a technically malfunctioning Sec Unit forming itself a family out of humans that treat it like a person due to their own biases, those humans' own families, as well as a ship that it's not ready to admit it loves. (It's all very complicated and full of human emotions and sometimes, one may feel the need to go stare at a wall for a while to deal with all of the things that need to be dealt with. Or to push them to the side. Either works.)

Obviously, this is hardly a comprehensive list of books or authors that have dealt in families, and for example, sibling relationships are entirely missing from this exploration, but these are books that had an effect on my thinking about family in science fiction. And where better to start than with the trope of found families?

The blood of the covenant

One of my bigger pet peeves is sayings that are being used to suggest the complete opposite of their actual meaning. Pulling yourself up by your bootstraps is impossible by definition. I'm sure more or less everyone's heard "Blood is thicker than water", but how many know that the full saying is "The blood of the covenant is thicker than the water of the womb"?[2] There's something to say for the people that you choose to have in your life, the people who choose you with all your quirks and issues to be in their lives. Certainly science fiction writers from Robert A. Heinlein to Octavia Butler to Starhawk to Charlie Jane Anders have spilled a lot of ink over the various aspects of chosen family. And for good reason. Making our own families is part of the process of growing up, and unsurprisingly there's a significant amount of literature of all kinds dedicated to that experience, whatever age it happens in.

The most common type of chosen family in most fiction is the romantic partner type, with optional kids. The most common of those, of course, being a one man and one woman type of relationship, like in *Old Man's War*. It's so common that it's almost considered a plot twist if that doesn't happen. Often there's extra plot points involved in trying to get there. In Scalzi's *Old Man's War*, the very existence of Jane Sagan is a plot point all to itself. John Perry, the protagonist, said goodbye to his wife, Kathy Perry, years earlier, when she died before her tour of duty with the Colonial Union could ever begin. So when, in the moment of his almost-death, he sees a green version of her, he is deservedly confused, but also certain that his dead wife has come to take him to the Great Beyond. Turns out, Kathy Perry provided her likeness and a significant chunk of her DNA to Jane Sagan, a Special Forces soldier, who is all of six years old when the two of them meet. Technically, the two of them have two meet-cutes; one where Perry is almost dead, and the other where Jane beats the snot out of him. But for all that, theirs is a very conventional romance. I could almost replace it with mine and my partner's; met at work, had a little difficulty getting started, but eventually became close and lived happily ever after. Me and my partner have yet to overthrow a borderline-fascistic system, but we're still young.

Moving on to the less conventional romances, Starhawk's family structures in *The Fifth Sacred Thing* are interesting because they are chaotic. There are the happy polycules containing multiple genders, with and without kids. Men-only and women-only families, sometimes families with one couple and their kids. There's also one woman and her hareem of men. And all of the families are built upon everyone's consent to stay in that situation, to some extent including the children. This is in stark contrast to the dystopian Stewards and their society of strict rules enforced on everyone, regardless of their consent. There's a certain familiarity, at least to me, in Starhawk's imagined future. That could be because there are so many polyamorists in my circle, as well as a lot of people who find consent really important. Starhawk's imagined future is also one that I, personally, find really plausible for humanity. Having multiple adults in a household, whether that be multiple generations or many adults of the same age has, after all, been the primary mode of humanity for millennia. The 'two adults and two and a half kids and a picket fence' is super recent as a way of living, and especially since the pandemic, it doesn't seem like it's working for anyone. In this economy, who can even afford it?

Butler's Xenogenesis goes another way entirely. Pretty much the entirety of Butler's body of work is about examining hierarchies, and a significant point of the Xenogenesis series is about examining the ways that hierarchical thinking has led and is leading to the downfall of the human race. The interesting thing is that the Oankali, the aliens that come to save the dregs of humanity from a nuclear winter, fall into some of the same traps of hierarchical thinking by deciding that they know better than humans what humans need. And they take decades to discover that they are wrong. Over the course of decades, spanning the entire Xenogenesis series, the Oankali discover the ways that they have been wrong when the human-Oankali hybrids reach maturity, and manage to convince the Akjai[3] Oankali to allow an Akjai human colony on Mars. And while the Oankali treat their children with kindness, they are nevertheless treated as lesser beings who cannot yet fully advocate for themselves, let alone other people. That, to me, is an interesting contrast to Starhawk's consent-based situation. And thoughts around hierarchies are an interesting way to explore a family unit. In a way, Butler's Oankali wind up recreating a family hierarchy, just instead of the top-down view that might look familiar to current humans, it's more of a wheel-and-spoke model, with the ooloi in the middle of two pairs of different species people. The ooloi is also a necessity to make a child in Oankali society, and that includes the human-hybrid portions of Oankali society. A significant chunk of humans rescued from the blighted Earth refuse this situation, and thus form their own societies on the restored Earth. Butler winds up exploring both models of family in some very interesting ways.

While the romantic relationships many of us form are important in so many ways, there's another way that our chosen families shape us in science fiction, and that is by helping us form the people we become.

Fashioned creatures, half made up

While the Xenogenesis series explores whether we stay human when we mix with aliens, Charlie Jane Anders' *Victories Greater Than Death* explores the ways that drawing together keeps us human. We are, after all, a social species, and we need others around us to feel fully human. This is very much something that every single author I read for this essay seems to agree upon. In *Victories Greater Than Death* (and wow that is a long title when you start writing it out over and over) Tina gets called to leave Earth, as she always knew she would be, but what she did not expect was that her best friend, Rachel, would be drawn along with her – and multiple other Earth teenagers as well. Tina naturally feels protective of them, and they form their own little Earthling clique, because this is, after all, a YA novel. And ultimately, they become a little chosen family. They're all close with the alien crew they work with, but they're close with them like they would be with good colleagues. With each other, they form family bonds.

The same goes for Martha Wells' Murderbot. It is adamant about not being a human. It does not want to admit that its human parts need connection, but connections do happen, through soap operas and actual relationships with humans and other intelligent beings. Wells does a wonderful job of showing that Murderbot is deeply in need of connection with other sentient beings, that it feels like some are more sentient than others, and that it wants and needs the company of some over others. Even as the narrator itself is literally insisting that it neither wants nor needs anything of the sort, and in fact, wants and needs the complete opposite. Nowhere is this as evident as in *System Collapse*, which is the latest book in the series. Dr Mensa's child is on an expedition with Murderbot, and she makes sure that both Murderbot and ART, a sentient ship Murderbot met in an earlier book, talk things through in order to come to some form of resolution to an argument they're having. It's honestly kind of cute, even. But the point is that without really knowing it, Murderbot is using its chosen family as a way to explore what it means to be a person, even though it is adamantly not a human.

And, really, that brings us back to Xenogenesis. The human and the Oankali come together to make the construct children, who try to explore both sides of their heritage; the human side tends to be explored more, given that they are on Earth to make sure that the human race survives as part of the Oankali and move into the future. The very first woman to start forming the human race into their future form, Lilith, becomes the mother of the protagonists of the next books and she herself thinks about the future of humanity a lot as well as her own place and responsibility for it. She has conflicting feelings about both: she winds up going with the Oankali plan and also being mad about it. And she's not entirely alone in that. Beyond the previously mentioned resisters, Lilith's children also have significant issues with the arrangement. Not least when the first male child born to a human gets kidnapped by the resisters, and spends a significant chunk of his first years with them, permanently losing his connection to the Oankali society in a way that leaves him cut off from his family. It is no surprise, then, that he winds up being the one to argue for the human race to have a chance on their own, without the Oankali. His book is also the one that I found myself identifying most with. The Oankali do some terrible things to the humans, because they cannot find it in themselves to see some of the harm they're doing while they're also helping. To me, personally, as someone who has never even wanted kids, the most terrifying part of the pairing with the Ooloi is that it leaves the romantic partners unable to touch each other except through the Ooloi, even non-romantically. I'm very touchy-feely with the people I love, and never being able to so much as hug someone I love without an intermediary between us sounds entirely unbearable.

As I was reading *Dawn*, I found myself thinking about the Romanian orphans under Ceaușescu. Without getting into the actual abuse, after abortion was banned in Romania in

1966, there was such an influx of abandoned infants that orphanage staff couldn't handle it. So even the children whose needs for sustenance and basic safety were met were hardly ever held by another human. As a result, they developed a lot of self-soothing mechanisms that were more often than not diagnosed as various forms of mental illness. Even in adult humans, touch starvation can lead to anxiety, stress, and depression. While the humans who've mated with an Ooloi can still touch the Ooloi and their children, they can't touch another adult who has mated with an Ooloi. And since the entire adult Oankali society is mated with an Ooloi, they can't touch any adult but their Ooloi. That sounds awful to me. It's an aspect that is not explored in the books beyond the initial shock, but it is the one I find myself returning to a few weeks after my last reread. Also on that note, Murderbot is obviously a person. And yet, it doesn't like to touch others unless absolutely necessary. So obviously being able to touch others is not necessary for personhood or being a member of a family. Heck, I definitely know people who are touch-averse and no less persons for it. But even so, in all of the examples that I reread for this essay, there is something in their respective families that helps the protagonists ground themselves as human. Even John Perry, when he has a meltdown because he doesn't feel human anymore, talks about being married as having an anchor, knowing where he belongs.

Tell my wife I love her very much, she knows

Science fiction is and always has been primarily a window to the present. Sure, there's always a bunch of cool things that we don't have now, but we could. The communicators from *Star Trek* providing the idea for cell phones is one of my favorite examples of that. Families in science fiction, I think, are both a window into today but also an imagining of what could be. Personally, I think that the actual likelihood is that as we move into the future, it's going to be more common for multiple generations to live together for many, many reasons, among which are both the changing economy and the scarcity of livable real-estate, especially as we start moving permanently off Earth. Forming a common purpose can be another reason for us to draw together. Also, in order to keep having children while both parents are working, we're going to need someone to be able to watch the children.[4]

In the end, I think that family, as a concept, is in the process of changing right now. The abandoned queer people are coming together, single mothers tired of their husbands weaponizing incompetence forming families with their friends, and elder members of the family are moving in because elder care is getting so expensive. At this point, it seems, at least to me, pretty safe to say that the one man, one woman, and 2.5 kids and a golden retriever model of family is on its way out. We can find inspiration from fiction for what's to come or we can figure out something else, something entirely different. And I, for one, look forward to seeing both the actual future as well as the science fiction that comes out of the changes that the future brings.

NINA NISKANEN WRITES SCIENCE FICTION, fantasy, and horror. She lives in Helsinki, Finland, with her partner, and her dog where she works as a computer programmer. She is passionate about space, language, textile arts, and creepy crawlies. She's a graduate of Viable Paradise and Clarion UCSD. More at ninaniskanen.com.

---

1. A group of non-monogamous people closely connected through romantic relationships ranging from simple (A is consensually dating both B and C who are not dating each other) to very complex (A is dating B and C, B is married to D, and also dating A and E, D is married to B and also dating C.)
2. Thanks to a commenter, I checked this again and could not find evidence that this was actually the original phrasing. Wikipedia (https://en.wikipedia.org/wiki/Blood_is_thicker_than_water) is the most concise source that I could find, but all the sources that mention that there is no actual evidence for this being the original framing do seem to agree that the two men mentioned by Wikipedia are the source of this claim. From Wikipedia: "Writing in the 1990s and 2000s, author Albert Jack[18] and Messianic Rabbi Richard Pustelniak, claim that the original meaning of the expression was that the ties between people who have made a blood covenant (or have shed blood together in battle) were stronger than ties formed by "the water of the womb", thus "The blood of the covenant is thicker than the water of the womb". Neither of the authors cite any sources to support their claim." Again, thanks to the commenter who pointed out my mistake.
3. The Oankali are a species of people who travel all of space in generationships, and when they meet other species, they persuade some of that species to grow a new ship with them and become a hybrid species that is still called Oankali. The Oankali call this trade. Usually some portion of both species is left out of the trade, and that portion is called Akjai. The Akjai Oankali from each trade go away on the ship they arrived in to find new trade elsewhere, once the trade is complete, and the new Oankali go away on the new ship they've grown together with the new hybrid species.
4. And speaking of children, the other thing that I had a hard time finding in science fiction was siblings. Lots of siblings in fantasy, with the Tensorate series coming to mind first. But that is another essay. There are mentions in science fiction of siblings existing, there are parental relationships. Could not think of any sibling relationships that I wanted to return to or even get recommendations to read for the first time. That is definitely something we as writers of science fiction should fix.

2

ROMANTIC LEAD BALLOONS

ANTI-ROMANCE AND MASCULINITY IN THE DISCWORLD

TANSY RAYNER ROBERTS

THIS ARTICLE CONTAINS spoilers for *Mort* (1987), *Pyramids* (1989) and *Moving Pictures* (1990). And *Gone with the Wind*. And *Speed*.

THE DISCWORLD HAS an odd relationship with romance. I recently discovered the novels of PG Wodehouse (fell down the rabbit hole a year ago, read 30+ novels at once, everything's fine, don't send help), an experience which feels rather like performing an archaeological dig on all British humour of the 20th Century.[1] I found myself delighted and charmed by this new reading experience, and immediately drew a whole lot of pencil lines between Wodehouse and Pratchett. If one of the things you love most about Discworld novels is the way that the author can describe the same situation twelve completely different times using such a complex and clever array of words that you want to turn his opening paragraph into a quilt and hug it forever, you'll probably get a real kick out of Wodehouse.

One of the big differences? Romance. Chaps in Wodehouseland are constantly falling in and out of love with girls, girls are likewise constantly falling in and out of love with chaps, and the only ones who aren't desperate to haul their favourite person to the nearest vicar for a quickie wedding are those who are desperately trying to avoid doing so with the wrong person (or, in the case of Bertie Wooster, trying to avoid doing so with literally anyone so he can remain married to Jeeves for the rest of his natural life).

In the Discworld, romance is... well, it's not very romantic. There are a few splendid couples forged over the course of the novels, and I will reluctantly admit to some stunningly romantic moments here and there.[2] However, these are the exception rather than the rule. Characters who are attracted to each other in the Discworld most often express this by being terribly embarrassed about it, insulting or being insulted by the other person, and in many cases, saying and doing nothing about their feelings until the plot turns around at the end to stomp on the romantic spark until it's well and truly snuffed out.[3]

This pattern was set by Rincewind[4] but many of the leading men of the Disc don't have the excuse of being technically celibate. They're just exceptionally bad at talking to girls.

Let's consider three of the Disc's hottest young bachelors, and discuss how these leading men of their respective novels fare in the romance department... and then, for good measure, I'm going to throw in a wild card and tell you who I think is actually the most romantic Discworld bloke. The answer might surprise you!

(No, it's not Vimes.)[5]

Bachelor #1 - Mort (*Mort*)

The early books of the Discworld feature such protagonists as Rincewind the wizard (definitely not interested in that scary dragon lady and/or dryad who just took her clothes off because magic is sexier than people), Esk (a 10 year old girl with no romantic ambitions) and Granny Weatherwax (none of your business). The closest we get to a successful courtship is the side quest of Cohen the Barbarian to rescue and eventually marry the handmaiden Bethan so she can tend him in his declining years (mm, swoony). It's only with *Mort* (1987) that we are treated to a proper Discworld romantic arc... which is to say, the novel introduces the concept of a romantic pairing, regularly undercuts the very concept of romance between that pairing, and makes both young people pretty miserable in the process.

We're constantly told how unattractive both Mort and Ysabell are — him with his knobbly knees and twitchy personality, she with her chocolate-induced curves and tendency to be rude to everyone.[6] He's 16 and so is she... but she has been 16 for decades, an awkward age-gap situation that is not questioned nearly enough.[7] They don't enjoy each other's company, and even worse, are thrown together by her father (Death) specifically so they will fall in love, which should suck any crumb of real romance out of the atmosphere.

(In addition, Mort spends most of the book crushing on a completely different girl.)

Somewhere along the way, the snark turns into banter, and Mort and Ysabell begin to care for each other. Stockholm Syndrome? Maybe. Like Keanu Reeves and Sandra Bullock in *Speed*, their intense situation forges something that eventually looks like a potential relationship... and the author finally throws us a grudging bone with a very dramatic scene towards the end Mort where Mort & Ysabell go through the motions of a Big Romantic Climax. We can at least believe in the pair as friends and allies after, if not properly In Love.

That's all we get. We never see them as a couple; their tragic early death in the opening of *Soul Music* (1994) takes them out of the Discworld too quickly. Most of what we learn about their married life is through their daughter Susan's recollections of the caution her parents felt about the supernatural world (i.e. Death).

All in all, not very satisfying. The book is brilliant, but the romance? Lukewarm at best.

ROMANCE: 3/8 upturned hourglasses

Anti-romance highlights: Ysabell compares Mort's chest to a toast rack in a wet paper bag; he responds (though does not say aloud) that the top of her dress contains "enough puppy fat for two litters of Rottweilers."

Bachelor #2 - Teppic AKA Pteppicymon XXVIII (*Pyramids*)

This young man is not only heir and later king of the wealthy, ancient kingdom of Djelibeybi, but his education at the Assassin's Guild renders him slightly suave, reasonably talented, and sartorially elegant. We soon learn, however, that while Flirting with Ladies is an important skill in the curriculum, Teppic remains inexperienced with sex or romance — especially in comparison to his confident friend, Chidder. Worst of all, when Teppic is unexpectedly pulled back home thanks to the death of his father, he learns (apparently for the first time) that aunts are not off the table when royal marriages are arranged.

Teppic immediately embarks on an incredibly romantic adventure to rescue the glamorous handmaiden Ptraci in his assassin persona after technically condemning her to death in his king persona. Once he assures himself that she wasn't that kind of handmaiden to his father (always important to check), the two pretty young people swashbuckle and bicker their way across the Djel, showing all the signs of falling in love and/or being the verge of some kind of epic romantic climax...

At which point, Teppic ditches her for his kingdom, then figures out she's his sister, then hands her the kingdom he never wanted in the first place, and attempts half-heartedly to matchmake her with Chidder on his way out...

In short, we have a romantic shaped storyline that closely resembles Lucy pulling the football away from Charlie Brown.

. . .

Romantic Success: 4/8 hungry crocodiles

Anti-romance highlights: Ptraci finding out how unglamorous it is to roll out of an antique carpet; their only kiss being fairly chaste and told from the point of view of a camel; BEING SIBLINGS.

Bachelor #3: Victor Tugelbend AKA Victor Maraschino (*Moving Pictures*)

Moving Pictures is one of the most romantic of the Discworld novels, with romance (especially the performative nature of romance) as a central theme. The Clicks are about romantic ideals, and the story explores what happens when appearance and artifice are prioritised over reality.

Victor and Ginger have all the elements of a classic screwball comedy couple: they're both attractive, she has plenty of reasons to be annoyed by him, they keep getting drawn together by circumstance, and there are plot tasks to work on together so the reader can see how compatible they are.[8]

The genuine potential of Victor and Ginger connecting on a romantic level is squeezed dry like an orange in a juicer thanks to external pressures. Dibbler and Silverfish (representing all terrible film studio heads ever) fall over themselves to invent a showmance between their leading man and lady, while the eldritch forces of Holy Wood literally take consent and free will out of their hands to push the couple together. The first time they kiss, neither Victor nor Ginger are conscious, because Holy Wood has taken over their bodies to act out a romantic fantasy for the Clicks.

We spend a lot of time inside Victor's head, and yet it's never 100% clear if he's even attracted to Ginger, or merely noticing features that a random observer might consider attractive. It's notable that their big final film is based on *Gone With the Wind*, a famous "romantic" epic featuring spousal abuse and the couple not ending up together.

In their final scene, Victor and Ginger feel more like friends who have survived a battle than two people who ever plan to kiss again — which is fine, it's actually kind of lovely that Ginger in particular is not defined by whether or not she's available to smooch the hero. Victor liking her as a person is a genuinely nice place to end the story after all the bickering and near-fatal encounters. But considering Victor and Ginger have spent the entire book being dragged through the structure of a romantic comedy, it's both fascinating and frustrating that this final scene gives no clue as to where they fall on the romantic/platonic scale.

I ship it. I've always shipped it. But we never learn what happens to either of them after Holy Wood ends! Then again, one might argue that finally getting a little privacy is the best possible romantic outcome for a celebrity couple...

Romantic Success: 6/8 banged grains

Anti-romance highlights: Neither of them remember their first kiss but she ends up with a mouthful of camel (what is it with Discworld anti-romance and camels?). When Viktor accidentally gets Ginger fired from the Clicks (meaning she'll have to return to milkmaiding) she yells at him: "Every time I see a cow's arse I'll think of you!"

AND OUR WILD CARD...

Bachelor #4: Detritus the Troll (*Moving Pictures*)

The most touching depiction of romance vs reality in this novel is not Victor and Ginger, but the courtship subplot of two trolls, Detritus and Ruby.

Detritus sets out to court Ruby in traditional troll fashion: choosing a large rock and hitting her over the head. She takes offence because Holy Wood's depiction of human-style romance has made her question her own cultural traditions.

Ruby insists that her swain performs her new definition of romance — and Detritus genuinely tries his best, bumbling through a new world of "pretty oograh" (she expects a bunch of flowers, he drags in a giant uprooted tree) or serenading his girl under a window (the noises he makes are truly appalling).

Detritus' failures are frustrating to Ruby, but so are her own natural instincts, which was against the artifice of the Clicks. Detritus, after all, fits the old-fashioned mould for "hunky troll," and she begins to regret pushing for a human-style romantic relationship when she secretly does just want to be bashed over the head and dragged into a cave.

This could be seen as playing into the problematic "women don't know what they really want" trope, but the point being made here is that cinematic depictions of romance can negatively impact real relationships. Ultimately, it's the fact that Detritus listens to what Ruby wants and tries to provide it that proves his love, not whether or not he's any good at it.

The final scene where Holy Wood magic allows Detritus to sweep Ruby off her feet... and she responds by hitting him over the head... cements them as one of the most genuinely romantic Discworld couples, no anti about it.

Romantic Success: 8/8 giant redwoods

Anti-romance highlights: Spurred on by Holy Wood, Ruby insists that a rock on the head might be quite sentimental, but diamonds are a girl's best friend; Detritus thinks she wants him to knock his own teeth out. And let's not forget what happens when she asks for sticky things to eat in a box and he dutifully ties a ribbon around a box containing a flayed horse...

Tansy Rayner Roberts is a Doctor of Classics, a Doctor Who podcaster, and an author of many science fiction and fantasy books, as well as the essay collection Pratchett's Women. *You can find her at tansyrr.com.*

---

1. At least, the subsection of British humour that relies on wordplay, banter, making fun of posh people, coming up with weirdly eccentric names for characters, getting one's heroes into amusing scrapes and/or forcing them to accidentally commit crimes. Let's say, 80%.
2. Moist Von Lipwig, for example, creates more than his fair share.
3. As discussed by me in Pratchett's Women, in essays such as "Have Scythe, Will Travel," exploring Susan's many truncated love stories.
4. Rincewind will get his own essay addressing his romantic dead ends and the celibacy of wizards later this year.

5. If you wish to remind yourself of some of Sam Vimes' greatest romantic hits, check out *Guards! Guards!* i.e. the book where he spends every interaction with Sybil Ramkin musing on how unattractive she is, or *Men at Arms*, the book in which he spends the days leading up to his wedding hating and resenting that it is happening at all. He turns out fine eventually, husband-wise, but he's not at any point a romantic lead.
6. Sadly, casual fatphobia and body shaming for "humorous" purposes is something else that the prose of both Pratchett and Wodehouse had in common – though to be fair, in the case of Mort and Ysabell the body shaming could be described as equal opportunity given how often both Pratchett and Ysabell have something mean to say about Mort's unattractive thinness.
7. Also not questioned enough: how can Ysabell gain weight in Death's Dominion if time stands still there and she cannot age? If she is the same weight as she was when first saved/abducted by Death then why the constant references to all the eating of chocolates and her extra curves as if the two have any relationship to each other?
8. Much like Teppic and Mort, Victor is given a leading man role in the story, while his potential romantic partner's point of view is rarely explored. Her character development mostly happens in conversation with him.

3

THE SEA IS WHOSE?

ETHNIC ENTANGLEMENTS IN SOUTHEAST ASIAN SFF

NG YI-SHENG

FOR YEARS NOW, I've been a passionate champion for Southeast Asian speculative fiction—just check out my *Strange Horizons* essay, "A Spicepunk Manifesto",[1] in which I praise its creation as a decolonial act. At the same time, I've struggled with an imbalance at the heart of this genre, obvious to insiders but otherwise almost invisible.

Simply put, the best-known authors of Southeast Asian SFF aren't racially representative of the region. We're ethnically Chinese. I'm talking about celebrated names like Zen Cho and Cassandra Khaw from Malaysia; Pim Wangtechawat and SP Somtow from Thailand; Jes and Cin Wibowo from Indonesia; Isabel Yap and Rin Chupeco from the Philippines; Neon Yang and Wen-yi Lee from Singapore; the editors of the landmark anthology *The SEA Is Ours,* Joyce Chng and Jaymee Goh—and myself, I guess, though I'm not that big on the celebrity scale. We're members of a diasporic community, constituting less than 5% of the 700 million-strong population of Southeast Asia,[2] but serving disproportionately as its cultural ambassadors.

One could argue that this isn't that big of a deal. Southeast Asians constitute a tenth of the world's population, just under the headcount of all of Europe. We're desperately underrepresented on the world stage—isn't it more important for *some* of us to be in the limelight than to quibble about whom?

Still, it's a little problematic when a Western reader picks up a copy of, say, *The Night Tiger* by Chinese Malaysian author Yangsze Choo, and assumes she has deep insider knowledge of the harimau jadian, the weretiger of indigenous Malay legend. Sure, she isn't utterly disconnected from this heritage, but the dynamic's comparable to a white South African's relationship to Zulu culture or a pākehā New Zealander's with Māori culture.

So, who gets to speak for Southeast Asia? Given our current state of representation, *how* do we speak about it? And if we agree this isn't ideal, what the hell do we do?

First off, let's address the whataboutisms. There *are* non-Chinese Southeast Asians who've made it big in Western publishing. Aliette de Bodard and Nghi Vo draw on their Kinh Vietnamese heritage in their *Xuya* and *Singing Hills* series;[3] Thea Guanzon does likewise as a Visayan from the Philippines with her *Hurricane Wars* series, and Hannah Alkaff as a Malay Malaysian with her middle-grade novels. Beyond genre SFF, there's also magical realists like Eka Kurniawan and Intan Paramaditha, both Javanese from Indonesia, plus Prabda Yoon and Pitchaya Sudbanthad, Thai from Thailand, all making their marks on global literary fiction.

Furthermore, there's plenty more ethnic diversity in national and regional publishing. According to Philippine authors Dean Francis Alfar, Victor Fernando R. Ocampo Jr. and Charles Tan, there's no significant pattern of Chinese dominance in their domestic SFF scene.[4] Even in my home country of Singapore—the only Chinese-majority nation in the region, where the term "Chinese privilege" is used as an analogue to white privilege[5]—there's been an explosion of Malay SFF writers since the 2010s, with folks like Nuraliah Norasid and Farihan Bahron winning recognition and awards for writing in both English and Malay. In his afterword to the anthology *Singa-Pura-Pura: Malay Speculative Fiction from Singapore,* editor Nazry Bahrawi describes "a sustained collective venture among authors of Malay descent in Singapore to experiment with the form productively.... a loose non-organised aliran (movement)."[6] However, he too points out the Chinese Singaporean dominance of the international scene, positioning the collection as a response to the question, "Where are the Malays?"[7]

Second, I think I'd better clarify how the Chinese stand in the complex racial dynamics of Southeast Asia. We're not foreigners: we're as authentically representative of our region as Black Americans or Indian Trinidadians are of their own nations, and even appear as characters in early indigenous epic literature like *Sulalatus Salatin* and *Serat Centhini*. Nor are we the descendants of colonists (unless you want to quibble about the case of Vietnam six hundred years ago). Our ancestors came largely as blue-collar workers and merchants from the mid-19th to early 20th centuries, and many were active in the nationalist struggles against European colonialism.

After independence, however, Chinese Southeast Asians became scapegoats of xenophobic movements—witness the anti-Chinese massacres in Malaysia in 1969 and in Indonesia in 1965 and 1998; also the mass expulsions from Vietnam in the 1970s and 80s. Consequently, there's a culture of insecurity and vigilance that's emerged, even in my home country of Singapore.[8] We've developed a mania for capital accumulation, higher education, the fostering of ties with other members of the Chinese diaspora, all so we can be protected or emigrate in case of violence. We've toxically embraced the racist moniker, "Jews of the Orient", coined for us by Vajiravudh, King of Siam.[9]

At the same time, many have also chosen the route of assimilation. In the Philippines and Thailand, the Chinese have intermarried and blended their cultures so much with native populations that it's often hard to distinguish who's whom. In Singapore, Malaysia and Indonesia, descendants of earlier waves of Chinese immigration have distinguished themselves as Peranakans, celebrating their syncretized culture as evidence of their national belonging. A few of us have even proven their loyalty by becoming prominent scholars of local history, such as Hsu Yun Tsiao of Singapore, Ong Hok Kam of Indonesia, Khoo Kay Kim of Malaysia.

All this means the Chinese of Southeast Asia are disproportionately wealthy, educated, proficient in English, knowledgeable about heritage and connected to global communities. These are privileges that arose out of trauma, and they're by no means consistent throughout the community. But they're privileges nonetheless, and they've translated handily into advantages in global SFF publishing.

Third—and yes, I'm still trying to impose numerical order on this section of my essay—the marginalization of non-Chinese voices leads to some thorny questions about how and what we write. Crucially, how do issues of cultural appropriation weigh against cultural representation?

The "stay in your lane" approach to avoiding appropriation doesn't work so well in the current Southeast Asian SFF scene. Sure, it can yield great books like Yangsze Choo's *The Ghost Bride* and Zen Cho's *The Order of the Pure Moon Reflected in Water*, both of which are specifically based on the histories and customs of the Chinese Malaysian community. Yet it also invites a withdrawal from regional representation. Sue Lynn Tan's *Daughter of the Moon Goddess* and Shelley Parker-Chan's *She Who Became the Sun* are set in fantastical versions of imperial China, and they're wonderful works—but it's only from the back matter that one may learn the authors are of Chinese Malaysian descent.

Chinese Southeast Asians do not need to confine ourselves to telling ghetto-ised stories. We are, as I said, authentic citizens within our own nations, and have a right to draw on our common cultural touchstones. Consider the case of the pontianak: an iconic vampiress of Malay horror. Despite her origins in indigenous folklore, she's part of a shared cosmopolitan tradition of storytelling: her first cinematic appearances, in films like *Pontianak* (1957) and *Anak Pontianak* (1958), were made respectively by Indian director BN Rao and Filipino director Ramon Estella, under Chinese production houses Cathay and Shaw Brothers. Today she's still believed in and feared by diverse communities across Malaysia, Singapore, Brunei and Indonesia.

This is why it was relatively uncontroversial for Zen Cho to write "The House of the Aunts", featuring a family of ethnically Chinese pontianaks. Notably, she pays homage to the Malay lore of the pontianak in her story—that they're created when women die during pregnancy; that they can be tamed with a nail in the back of their necks—and she features a major Malay character in the story, Ridzual, her protagonist's love interest. She's able to provide her own perspective on the pontianak legend without erasing Malayness.

Compare this to Yangsze Choo's aforementioned novel, *The Night Tiger*. My quarrel with it isn't that it draws on Malay legends of the weretiger, but that it does so without any Malay major characters—a phenomenon I've snarkily called yellow-washing: an analogue of whitewashing, when our multiethnic societies are portrayed as completely, or almost completely, Chinese.[10] By foregrounding Chinese and white characters' perspectives with global readers, the author's rendering the Malay population—the source culture for her legend, and the majority race of Malaysia—almost invisible.

Fortunately, Southeast Asian SFF authors tend to affirm rather than erase our region's ethnic diversity.[11] Jes and Cin Wibowo's *Lunar Boy* features a cast of mostly dark-skinned characters of indigenous Indonesian heritage, with the love interest Noah as its only prominent Chinese Indonesian character. Neon Yang's *Tensorate* series, though full of Chinese and Japanese-coded cultural elements, features the Indian-coded rebel Thennjay and the Malay-coded investigator Sariman. Non-Chinese authors do this too: Hanna Alkaff's *The Girl and the Ghost* pairs the Malay schoolgirl protagonist Suraya with a Chinese best friend, Jing Wei.

Does this spirit of anti-racism in storytelling correlate with a desire for a more racially varied slate of writers? My belief is that it does. Harking back to the anthology *The SEA Is Ours*: despite the fact that both editors Jaymee Goh and Joyce Chng were of Chinese descent, nine of the twelve chosen contributors were non-Chinese, including Filipina Kate Osias, Indonesian Ivanna Mendels and—making their début—Vietnamese-American Nghi Vo. It's part of why we choose to call ourselves Southeast Asian writers, rather than splitting ourselves into national or ethnic sub-groups. We're bound together by a belief in that diversity is strength.

So there's already will for change, even among the most privileged of us.

How do we actually make it happen?

LET's say you're a literary agent, a publisher, an editor or a festival organiser. You're in an unusual position of power. Beyond simply platforming BIPOC authors, you can make a conscious decision to include non-Chinese Southeast Asian writers—folks like Anselma Prihandita from Indonesia, Kathrina Mohd Daud from Brunei, Vida Cruz and Joel Donato Ching Jacob from the Philippines, Tunku Halim and Golda Mowe from Malaysia, Suffian Hakim and Manish Melwani from Singapore, not to mention writers from the wider diaspora like Hoa Pham from Australia and Salinee Goldberg from the USA. (It's genuinely strange that Filipinos constitute the largest Southeast Asian diasporic community in Canada, the US, the UK, Australia and New Zealand, yet number so few in globally published SFF.)

If you're a non-Chinese Southeast Asian SFF writer yourself, there's a good chance you know the struggle better than I do, and that any advice I clumsily dispense will be patronising and/or misguided. What I *will* say is that it's incredibly valuable to be part of an international SFF community, whether it's through writing courses, convention meet-ups, or just making lots of friends on social media; that although querying for agents is hell, there's loads of journals out there that are genuinely interested in representing diverse authors, like *Clarkesworld, Strange Horizons, khōréō* and more; also that Western readers may, unfortunately, want quite different things from the readers within your own nation (there is, alas, considerable overlap between self-representation and exotica); and that if institutions won't work for you, you can often start them yourselves: your own writing group, your own anthology, your own journal. And yeah, I know I'm part of the problem too. I'm willing to listen to hear how I can do better.

And if you're a Chinese Southeast Asian writer, as I am… well, I understand if you've mixed feelings about this essay. In an ideal world, advocating for more opportunities for others wouldn't mean fewer opportunities for ourselves, but I've a horrible premonition some agent or editor will misinterpret my message and blithely decide to boycott our writing. It's bollocks, and runs counter to my mission of getting more recognition for all of Southeast Asian SFF. Still, it's a risk I'm willing to take. Our missing voices need to be acknowledged. Plus, I'm plain *tired* of us being misunderstood as just a slightly spicier variant of China.

So I'm asking us to be a little more conscious about inclusivity and exclusivity. If we want to form communities based on our Chinese diasporic identity,[12] that's cool, but we can be transparent about that—a fine example would be *Lauriat: A Filipino-Chinese Speculative Fiction Anthology*, edited by Charles Tan and featuring authors such as Isabel Yap, Paolo Chikiamco and Rin Chupeco. If we're thinking in terms of Southeast Asia, however, or any one of the multi-ethnic nations within, we need to consider who's being left out of the conversation and how it's possible to respectfully bring them in, by befriending them, reading them, promoting them, just as we'd do for any of our respected peers.

If you've the will and the talent, you might even want to try translation. One big reason why more Southeast Asian authors haven't broken into global publishing is that many of us are writing in local languages; many of us are fluent enough to be a bridge between them and the Anglophone world. Chinese Indonesian author Tiffany Tsao, once known for her *Oddfits* SFF series, now devotes much of her time to translating Indonesian language works by her countryfolk, such as *Happy Stories, Mostly* by Norman Erikson Pasaribu, who uses occasional speculative elements to shine a light on his life as a queer man from the Batak minority. I've made a stab at this myself, with an extremely amateur translation of Singaporean Malay language author Hassan Hasaa'ree Ali's "Schizosinga".[13] Yet there's also a danger here of taking opportunities away from non-Chinese translators, similar to global debates over white translators and translators of colour.[14] As it turns out, there aren't easy ethical workarounds for privilege.

There's a line I wrote in "A Spicepunk Manifesto", arguing that part of the "punk" of this regional movement should be "to ensure that if Southeast Asian authors are to prosper, then we must prosper together." It's a utopian ideal, and it extends to so many more topics than race—eventually we've gotta address inequities of class, gender, nationality, religion, disability status, immigration status and more.

But as a Chinese Singaporean in the scene, race feels like as good a place as any to start. I want to hear more stories by Southeast Asians who don't look the same as myself or my biological family. And I want the whole damn world to hear these stories too.

GREAT THANKS *to Daryl Qilin Yam, Nazry Bahrawi, Victor Fernando R. Ocampo Jr., Dean Francis Alfar and Charles Tan for their insights and advice on this essay.*

NG YI-SHENG IS A SINGAPOREAN WRITER, *researcher and activist with a keen interest in Southeast Asian history, literature and myth. He is the author of the SFF collection* Lion City *and formerly co-organised IndigNation: Singapore's Pride Season and the Southeast Asian Queer Cultural Festival. His website is* ngyisheng.com.

---

1. Ng Yi-Sheng, "A Spicepunk Manifesto: Towards a Critical Movement of Southeast Asian Heritage-Based SFF." *Strange Horizons.* 29 August 2022. http://strangehorizons.com/non-fiction/a-spicepunk-manifesto-towards-a-critical-movement-of-southeast-asian-heritage-based-sff/
2. It's tricky to get clear numbers, but Leo Suryadinata calculates 26.872 million Chinese Southeast Asians using statistics from 2010 and earlier. Divided by a total Southeast Asian population in 2010 of 593 million, that puts our percentage around 4.53%. Leo Suryadinata, "A Rising China Affects Ethnic Identities in Southeast Asia." *ISEAS Perspective*: Issue 2021, No. 74.

3. Kinh writers like De Bodard and Vo may still be said to reap the benefits of light-skinned privilege, but I fear I don't have the cultural knowledge to properly discuss this topic.
4. Tan clarifies that many Philippine writers are of partial Chinese descent but are not raised with Chinese culture, and also notes the tendency of those raised with Chinese culture to be beneficiaries of class and wealth privilege. Significantly, he states, "there aren't a lot of Philippine science fiction and fantasy that deal with specific Filipino-Chinese concerns." Email correspondence, 29 October 2024.
5. For more on Chinese privilege in Singapore, see "Chinese Privilege, Gender and Intersectionality in Singapore: A Conversation between Adeline Koh and Sangeetha Thanapal." *Boundary 2*. 4 March 2015. https://www.boundary2.org/2015/03/chinese-privilege-gender-and-intersectionality-in-singapore-a-conversation-between-adeline-koh-and-sangeetha-thanapal/
6. Nazry Bahrawi. "Malays Speculating Futures." *Singa Pura-Pura: Malay Speculative Fiction from Singapore*. Ed. Nazry Bahrawi. Ethos Books: 2021. P184.
7. Ibid. p. 175.
8. This is true even in Singapore, where paranoia persists about being a Chinese-majority nation surrounded by mostly Malay Muslim neighbours. Furthermore, there've been patterns of discrimination within the Chinese community: the government has historically been dominated by Anglophone Chinese who've disenfranchised Sinophone political and intellectual movements. See Hong Lysa and Huang Jianli. *The Scripting of a National History: Singapore and Its Pasts*. NUS Press, 2008.
9. I've been unable to access a copy of the infamous essay myself, which was published in 1914 in both English and Thai. However, it's cited in numerous texts, e.g. Benedict Anderson. *Imagined Communities: Reflections on the Origin and Spread of Nationalism*. Verso, 2006. P. 100.
10. In a Singaporean context, the most prominent example of yellow-washing in genre fiction is in the field of romance rather than SFF. Kevin Kwan's *Crazy Rich Asians* and its film adaptation portray Singapore as an almost wholly Chinese country, where the most prominent non-Chinese characters of Asian descent are servants and South Asian security guards. See Hannah Ellis-Petersen and Lily Kuo. "Where are the brown people? Crazy Rich Asians draws tepid response in Singapore." *The Guardian*. 21 August 2018. https://www.theguardian.com/film/2018/aug/21/where-are-the-brown-people-crazy-rich-asians-draws-tepid-response-in-singapore

11. Readers may notice I haven't accused Chinese Southeast Asians of racism. It's definitely true that racism and colourism exist in the community, especially in Singapore, where Chinese like myself are the majority. But in the rest of Southeast Asia, the minority status of the Chinese, and the high variation in the degree of their cultural assimilation, makes the issue more complicated, since it doesn't overlap clearly with hegemonic state power.
12. There are in fact academics specifically studying the literature of Chinese Southeast Asians, much of it on the SFF spectrum. See Brian Bernards. *Writing the South Seas: Imagining the Nanyang in Chinese and Southeast Asian Postcolonial Literature*. NUS Press, 2016.
13. Hassan Hasaa'ree Ali, "Schizosinga". *Singapore Unbound*. November 3, 2023. https://singaporeunbound.org/suspect-journal/2023/11/3/schizosinga
14. See Alex Marshall. "Amanda Gorman's Poetry United Critics. It's Dividing Translators." *The New York Times*. 26 March, 2021. https://www.nytimes.com/2021/03/26/books/amanda-gorman-hill-we-climb-translation.html

4

UNTANGLING QUIET

E.D.E. BELL

I've always been an empath, though I didn't know it for a long time. And I've been writing as long as I could do so, nearly all speculatively. This exploration through writing was always at the core of my being, in the ways that my ability to *feel* shaped my need to *connect* and to *lift*, but it was always shunned. Not by an industry or editors; I didn't get that far for decades. But by the community around me, who told me that to survive, I needed to focus on the practical. On control. Toughness. Not whimsy or fantasy.

Now, looking back, I can also say that I've always been drawn not only to reading and writing in general but to quiet fiction—stories focusing on introspective and interconnecting tension—most of all, though I didn't know it had a name.

Then I met professors. (Strongly recommended, though endearing side-effects may occur.) I remember listening to Carlos Hernandez talk about how quiet fiction is, in many ways, the oldest fiction—how shepherds with much time to themselves would sit and ponder and tell stories of the universe from the perspective of one or two—but that it was not sought by today's industry.

Which got me thinking: Why was this form of fiction, which had a name, and was not just a known thing but an ancient thing, being pushed away to the point of almost not being talked about? A rejection not even based on whether it could make money, but a specific aversion across speculative genres by those in control.

Over time, I saw it very clearly.

Quiet Fiction is *powerful*.

All fiction is powerful, all storytelling is powerful, all art, all creation is powerful. But Quiet Fiction cuts right to our heart. It is empathy. It is connection. It is the stories that have started and ended wars, the stories that have brought peace to troubled hearts, and fire to dry kindling.

Louder fiction is powerful also, but I think, as the external is generally easier to keep more active and more visual (say, a battle), it is more possible to draw the focus away from messages of empathic human connection or structural harm, or at least keep them subtle enough not to sway—or to irritate. To do so for reasons of stifling those messages, but also just plain financial risk. (The two are, of course, deeply related.) This shifting, softening, can be done in many cases without the readership knowing it. (I note the recurring discussion about focus groups shaping movies to be less objectionable to anyone.) Whereas in a quiet work, when pain or connection or joy is unwrapped, it is harder to make a softened version appealing.

This is why I think our language regarding fiction, in this case regarding genre labels, is so important.

Once I understood Quiet Fiction was a known and ancient thing, I spent a few years talking to scholars and readers about it, until I felt pretty comfortable in understanding that it was more internally based, and had mostly let the topic settle in my mind. Then my interest in broader categorization was sparked with a burst of writers talking cosy / cozy all of the sudden. After that when I would say "quiet" people would ask, "Oh, cozy?"

Then "gentle" got brought into it. "Oh, cozy?"

The blending of these concepts bothered me, so I started talking about Quiet Fiction, now from this new angle. Sure, I didn't want to say "quiet" or "gentle" about our press' work and have "NWL" be heard (as in nice white lady, as in nothing that might make someone uncomfortable, which is not at all our aim), but it felt important at broader levels, also, related to the softening of louder fiction. Perhaps Cozy was even a way to feed the growing appetite for connection among readers without letting Quiet take hold.

In 2023, I was speaking on a panel at Can*Con about quiet fiction and discussed this concern, and Suzan Palumbo asked a question from the back row of the audience. (I tried not to act starstruck when I saw her.) Later, online, she talked about related issues and said she found the discussion on cozy a bit funny, really, because it is "defined by white people."

I thought about this *a lot*.

And also got thinking, yeah, I read a book described as cozy and found it actually pretty uncomfortable. So what help is a label that leads people to the wrong books, especially one specifically offering some form of safety? Is there nonetheless value in describing whether a murder story is cozy or not, for example?

I'm certainly not saying I have the answers, but I do love the discussion, think it's important, and am grateful for a place to continue it. It's also worth noting that genre terminology is fluid; it can be different in different cultures, and even collectively, may change in one or five or twenty years. And certainly, books may weave between or combine or move beyond genre labels.

Yet, I remain convinced, that especially now that we've re-popularized the concept of cozy in exploratory fiction (xpfic, my proposal for a broader, more globally-appropriate term than specfic), we should take care regarding when we use it.

And why.

With that background and understanding, I'll walk through the current reaches of my own contemplations. The labels I am putting forward are: Quiet, Gentle, Hopeful, and Mild.

So, first, why not cozy? The premise of Cozy Fiction is that painful themes are absent or not upsetting. Back to the Can*Con panel, the question that Suzan Palumbo asked there was about the idea of Cozy Horror. I answered at the time that I didn't have enough expertise in Horror to know. Nor do I now. But I asked Linda D. Addison about Horror this summer, and she told me that she believes Horror is meant to unsettle in some way, making Horror such a broad and interesting genre. And, it seems, more than a description. Is a cute spooky ghost story Cozy Horror, or only Cozy? I'd be very interested to hear the Horror community discuss this further, but in my own current thoughts, I keep considering that Cozy is best left as a way to describe *a read-*

er's experience than a genre label. That "I found this book so cozy" is more appropriate than "this is a cozy book". And that, to me, feels on a different scale than a concept like Horror, rather than two sides of a scale (so Horror could indeed be cozy, for an individual).

The four genre labels I am proposing here are:

Quiet Fiction: My love and my genre, so I've thought about this more than the others, and talked to every expert I've had opportunity to on the topic. I fumbled around definitions for a long time, but now consider the essence of Quiet Fiction to be **introspective including interpersonal tension**. *Not low-stakes* (any suggestion that internal stakes and decisions and paths are unimportant is being a voice to the oppressors, in my foot-stompy very opinionated opinion!) but introspective. Including our timelines, our connections. I have not heard a better contrasting term than **Loud**.

Gentle Fiction: Painful themes are written mindful of, and not with the goal to disturb, reader trauma. I first heard R.B. Lemberg explain this term as an intentional descriptor for fiction, and, yes, I would say their works are a perfect example of gentle writing. They write on some of the most serious of themes, ones that will surely be upsetting to the reader, and yet, the reader can feel safe with their writing. And then, what is the opposite? I will go with **Brutal**.

Hopeful Fiction: Fiction that depicts elements of hope in order to inspire readers. I believe this label *and its accurate application* are especially important in these times, especially in the context of what I consider its opposite: **Grim**.

An aside: During the popularized surge in Grim Fiction I was thinking about this a lot. On one hand, there was a rush to call things Grim that were not Grim. Or to equate Fantasy with Grim, which, honestly—really irked me. And then, when people started to feel a little prickly that, wait, wasn't Fantasy about hope and joy and why are we feeling a little icky right now, there was an entire conversation on *why* something is Grim. Is there some betterment of society involved in this story (and yes, I believe *every* story should benefit society; there is no neutrality in expression by the nature of expression), and otherwise why was it written? I personally use the phrase "The Martin Defense" for this… Sure, I'll say it. When a question is asked about whether content is actually harmful, and the answer is reduced to some form of obvious "realism," that is what I casually call The Martin Defense. (Yes, it could use a better term.)

Grim Fiction can be a powerful warning. A call to action. A thought exercise. An exploration. That is very different than harm being glorified or enjoyed.

And lastly, not so intriguing, but I do think useful, is the level of content itself.

Mild: The content, on whatever topic, is metered in the intensity and detail of its description. I think this one is probably more established, with the other side of the scale being **Graphic**. Yet I note it here to emphasize that mild or graphic content can rest anywhere on these other scales. Yes, this ties into specific content notes, but I think it's also useful for describing a book as a whole.

These labels hopefully clarify that one can write Loud, Brutal, Grim, and Graphic content without it being harmful. To put it another way: Harmful content cannot hide under our labels, once we have claimed their meanings.

Of the other terms I contemplated alongside these, I'd like to address a few of them: **Dark**, **Punk**, and **Clean**.

In this discussion of Grim, you may have noticed I omitted the -dark. So: about Light and Dark. I believe that there will always be value and deep meaning to humans in the exploration of light in darkness. Light creates visibility, and growth. Light is the Sun, the Moon, the Stars. Light is a good, necessary, and primal path to life itself. But given the extensive use of light colors in xpfic (and marketing and literary motifs well beyond) as a metaphor for good and dark colors as a metaphor for bad, as a device for normalizing greed through systemic racism— I'm thinking, with all these other labels, we just don't need (at a minimum) these terms at the genre level. Thus, a "Grimdark" book could be described as Grim, or Grim, Graphic, and Brutal, and make a very clear distinction between that, and a story which takes place in the shadows and may be deeply unsettling on serious topics but is actually written in a Gentle, Hopeful style.

X-punk Fiction: I know this has been an overloaded marketing term, but I think it is a term that we need. Again, if the term is used correctly. Punk exists against the establishment. Against oppression. Against control. And it would be very Punk to reclaim Punk from the shine of corporate marketing. The word itself was reclaimed from its origins of substandard, worthless, weak, sex work—*gay*. So my opinion is that we should protect punk with vigor, and use it for those topics. If it's not fighting the system, don't call it Punk. Perhaps the opposite would be... ***Safe***. To again quote

Suzan Palumbo, mostly because I find this a pretty succinct rallying call for our times, "You wanna be punk, you gotta be punk."

And finally, a quick note on **Clean Fiction**. There are issues with this term and many of the people who use it. But I also know that the label has been important to people of certain backgrounds, belief systems, and traumas, and so, I don't want to touch this one for now. As with the rest, I will be interested to see further discussion. (And **Dirty Fiction**, well, cheers.)

Of these four scales, described on one side as Quiet, Gentle, Hopeful, and Mild—while one of my main proposals is that these are separate, I think there is much value in discussing them together. And, yes, as a fantasy-loving nerd, I am always happy to ponder on topics of multidimensional data. In this case, my mind went to personality indices, such as Myers-Briggs. I don't really want to get into those here; they have a lot of issues, and I am not a psychologist.[1] It's not perfect, but the thought of four-axis, digitized, binary codes did seem like a first way to consider it.

Thus, we could have four scales:

I wonder how useful, or how damaging, it could be to code books this way, for purposes of communicating their content and focus. Perhaps we would use codes for a book strongly on one side, and omit any of the four where the book is not strongly weighted to one side.

I am saying this part less because I think it should be something we start using (proposing more clarity on the terms is the place I wanted to get to) but because showing them this way emphasizes that any combination of these is possible. And no combination is difficult to come up with, though some are certainly more what is being marketed and published. And none of these, in themselves, are "good" or "bad"—that's important.

In all this, context is essential. As I discussed in Apex Magazine Issue 143 "Escapism is a Lie", bins and their boundaries are necessary to oppression, as it becomes much harder to keep gates without walls. In these cases we must resist false choices: this *or* that. Yet labels are important to experience and expression. To individuals and communities, bins help us communicate, and walls help us *protect*. With any gate, then, the question is who is keeping that gate, and why.

I absolutely do feel an urgency to these discussions; I think we are in a unique place in time. Yes, the stifling of expression has gone on for millennia but the level of technology we are facing has not. I truly believe we are in the early stages (or at least we need to be) of what I call the indie re-revolution.

The first revolution was the turn of this century. As connections developed globally, there was a surge of the ability for people and organizations to communicate freely and independently.

Yet now, I am seeing—many are seeing—a system-wide crunch to stop that new, global level of power before we realize what we've lost, what possibilities have been blocked from our reach. And if you're feeling it, what you're feeling is violent. Aggressive. Intentional. This push toward monopoly, toward franchise, toward opportunity-forced niceness—some of us feel it pressing on our skin. And I have been surprised how *uncomfortable* this topic makes people, as if it's the essence of some performativity measure.

Perhaps it is.

I have been noticing a theme from the most respected exploratory authors of our day. Whether in posts, conversations, or set into the stories themselves: the direct statement —the reminder—that many things are possible. There has, I think always been a message at the core of fiction, whether inherent or meta, that our stories are not yet written, a day is not yet written, a far future is not yet written. But lately I've seen it stated more in solid form. Like a smooth rock one can hold in their hands. Whatever the odds, high or low: *Many things remain possible.*

Why do we read stories? Why do we tell stories? What is the uniting factor in every good story ever told, most certainly in exploratory fiction?

I think it is this: Whether as a warning, or to inspire hope, a story reminds us that possibilities remain. The coziest of cozy reading experiences can do this. As can the most unsettling.

And so, I truly believe we must talk about writing, publishing, and the language we use for both. Many of these topics are being reformed in a rapidly changing world.

And what is on the line is free human expression.

And that is existential.

I am grateful to Bogi Takács for nudging me to formalize my thoughts a bit more, to Alex Pierce and Speculative Insight

Journal for welcoming those thoughts, and to you for taking your time to read and consider them. I hope they will add sparks to continuing discussion. I would love to see it! With love and warmth from winter in Detroit...

E.D.E. BELL (SHE/HER or e/em) *is a fantasy writer and small press editor. A passionate vegan and earnest progressive, she feels strongly about issues related to equality and compassion. Eir works are quiet and queer and often explore conceptions of identity and community, including themes of friendship, family, and connection. She lives in Ferndale Michigan, where she writes stories, revels in garlic, and manages the creative side of her indie press, Atthis Arts. You can follow Emily's adventures at <u>edebell.com</u>.*

---

1. And yeah, I worked for a government office where every new participant was asked to take a personality test, then the Director's assistant (with benefits) would carry a little flip book so she could know how best to manipulate each person. I have so many stories... but I'm not here to talk about those.

5

CELIBACY & THE SINGLE WIZZARD

TANSY RAYNER ROBERTS

> When it comes to wine, women and song, wizards are allowed to get down and croon as much as they like. (*Sourcery*.)

WIZARDS DON'T HAVE SEX. Except of course where sex = biological gender because wizards are male in almost all instances and will argue any exceptions out of existence.

The celibacy of wizards is an odd quirk of Discworld magic which regularly returns as a running joke. However, most people (including the wizards themselves) are hazy on the 'why' behind the sex ban. Is 'No Sex Please, We're Wizards' a rule of the universe, a rule of Unseen University, or more of a guideline?

We're offered several answers over the course of the series, contradicting one another, and awash with flagrant heteronormativity. Marriage, sex and procreation in the Discworld are inevitable and interchangeable consequences, it seems, of men and women being allowed to come into contact with each other.[1]

The reasons given for the celibacy of wizards in the Discworld can be largely grouped into three categories:

1) Sexual expression and even sexual thoughts are literally incompatible with magic, and may affect a wizard's ability to perform.[2]

2) Wizards must be prevented from indulging in marriage and/or extra-marital sex to prevent procreation, with particular reference to the birth of Sourcerors.

3) Unseen University must be preserved as a wholly masculine space[3] so that the wizards may spend their days immersed in an academic Shangri-La of dusty books, magical duels, nine square meals a day and a constantly-replenishing cheese trolley without having to bother themselves about the potentially nagging or needy voices of wives, mothers or children.[4]

A fourth theory might be considered, implicit rather than explicit in the text: the men who are drawn to wizardry as a career are predominantly those who have little interest in or knowledge of sex in the first place, placing the imposed celibacy of wizardry somewhere between an irrelevance and a blessed relief.

---

1. Incompatibility

> The reason given to young wizards was that the practice of magic is hard and demanding and incompatible with sticky and furtive activities. It was a lot more sensible, they were told,

to stop worrying about that sort of thing and really get to grips with Woddely's Occult Primer instead. (*Sourcery*.)

It is often expressed across the Discworld novels that a wizard's magic is incompatible with sexual expression, romantic entanglement, or even lustful thoughts.

At the end of *Mort*, Ysabell hints at the burgeoning romance between the wizard Cutwell and Queen Keli, suggesting that he hasn't been seen doing much magic lately. Ysabell, of course, is not an expert — and her cheeky aside does not clarify whether Cutwell is choosing not to use magic, or can no longer perform magic, now that he and Keli are (allegedly) romantically involved.

This concept of wizarding practice being hampered by sexual impulses or activity is regularly alluded to by Rincewind, the first wizard (or rather, wizzard) we meet in the early Discworld novels.

Rincewind is established early on as the sort of chap who would be disastrous around women even were he not pledged to a profession that demands celibacy. Luckily, his interest in them is minimal at best. He is often thrown into the path of forthright, attractive young ladies in the manner of all protagonists of heroic fantasy, requiring Fate and/or the author to step in long before Rincewind genuinely has to choose between magic and sex.

Because, of course, he would choose magic.

In *The Light Fantastic*, Rincewind (prevented from learning spells thanks to the giant scary spell from the Octavo living rent-free in his head) finally experiences magic, if only remotely.

 Magic! So that was what it felt like. No wonder wizards didn't have much truck with sex! (*The Light Fantastic*)

He acknowledges that he's had orgasms in his time ("sometimes even in company") "but nothing from his experience got close, not even by far, with that hot, tensioned moment when every part of his body was invaded by the white-blue fire, when magic sprung out of his fingers."[5]

In *Sourcery*, Rincewind clearly believes the myth that sex would hurt his magical ability — during his brief window of fancying Conina, he briefly considers the unarguable fact that his magic is rubbish anyway, so what would he have to lose?

When Conina meets and instantly falls for Nijel (her actual love interest), Rincewind's dismay has far more to do with the inconvenience of two travel companions getting soppy than a personal sense of lost romantic opportunity. The main vibe he gives off is relief. Wild sourcery comes into his life shortly thereafter, and Rincewind spends the rest of the book thinking about magic instead of girls.[6]

---

2. The Prevention of Sourcery

Sourcery (1988) provides a whole new explanation for the wizarding sex ban. Here, we are told that it's not merely a bit naughty to break this particular rule... it might break the world.

Ipslore the Red was exiled from wizarding and the University "for daring to love" — which is to say, for marrying a woman. This would not have had any further consequences, had the couple not gone on to have eight sons. The youngest, Coin, as a third generation eighth son, automatically becomes a world-destroying magical force known as a Sourceror.

Sourcery explicitly states that no matter what else has been said on the topic (by the same author), the long-forgotten real problem is "if wizards were allowed to go around breeding all the time, there was a risk of sourcery."[7]

While it is true that birth control in a fantasy world (even one on the brink of a highly inventive industrial revolution, with an army of competent seamstresses ready to advise) is unlikely to be reliable, it is interesting that the fear of sourcery has given rise to such a drastic regulation for wizards.

All one would need, surely, is the distribution of a magical infertility charm to all student wizards, and the issue could have been solved.

It is only the practice of wizardry — an intellectual vocation for men involving books and the rote-learning of spells as compared to the more practical day-to-day magic performed by witches — that is considered incompatible with sex in the Discworld, which might go some way to explaining why the only decision witches need to make regarding sex or no sex is whether or not they wish to balance family *and* a career.[8]

When Archchancellor Ridcully re-visits the kingdom of Lancre in *Lords and Ladies*, he indulges in wistful, rose-coloured memories of 'the one that got away,' a lively girl who (it turns out) grew up to be Granny Weatherwax.

Ridcully remembers being at a crossroads as a young wizard, with magic no longer satisfying him. He briefly considered ditching wizardry to marry Esme, but their romance fizzled out. Ridcully now has a successful wizarding career — and yet, he indulges in wistful sighs about what might have been.

Granny is also haunted by the alternate universe in which she married Ridcully, had children, and so on… but unlike the wistful wizard, she has few regrets. Crucially, the version of Esme Weatherwax who married Ridcully could have continued as a witch, while he could certainly not have stayed a wizard. Had their lives gone down that path, Ridcully might easily have turned into another Ipslore the Red, given that quitting wizardry doesn't solve the Sourcerer problem.[9]

Despite *Lords and Ladies* being written and set several years after the events of Sourcery, Ridcully is casually unbothered about the potential consequences of a wizard indulging in sex, referring to that particular rule as being more of a guideline.

---

3. No Girls Allowed

CELIBACY & THE SINGLE WIZZARD   51

Just because the "true" reason for the ban on wizard sex stems from procreation rather than prudery, does not mean it is the only reason.

It has always been convenient to the wizarding community to ban marriage, sex and procreation from its members. The mystique of the wizarding profession includes an invitation to live within the gates of Unseen University in an eternal boys club: an old-fashioned masculine space where the only women allowed to enter are those doing the cooking or the cleaning, while minding their own business (as a wife, perhaps, could not be expected to do.)[10]

As early as *The Light Fantastic* (1986) we have a textual acknowledgement that the exclusion of women is for the selfish convenience of the male professors rather than any more logical purpose:

> Unseen University had never admitted women, muttering something about problems with the plumbing, but the real reason was an unspoken dread that if women were allowed to mess around with magic they would probably be embarrassingly good at it...

I recently came across a theory[11] that Tolkien's portrayal of the Ents was inspired by his wife's resentment of their life in Oxford where he thrived as an academic in the company of men including the Inklings, his awkward, intellect-obsessed male friend group. The Ents are slow, ponderous and vaguely melancholic about having been abandoned by the Ent-wives for no reason they can understand; this Inklings theory posits that the Ent-wives ditched their frustratingly intellectual husbands after years of having their own needs neglected.[12] If true, it shows a remarkable sense of self-awareness about Tolkien's strained relationship with his wife.[13]

There is certainly a long history of universities as havens for beardy bookish men to escape from their long-suffering wives and neglected children in order to play at being geniuses in an environment that rewards them with status, big dinners and fancy robes. Universities may have moved on from this old-fashioned concept but it was very much a Thing when Pratchett was writing his early Discworld books and dusty pockets of this style of academia can still be found on campuses today.

In *Equal Rites*, Unseen University's male-centred world does not allow for a girl like Esk, destined for wizardry by birth (the eighth daughter of an eighth son) to be accepted into their community. Granny spots the loophole immediately, showing Esk how to access the University unofficially by wielding a broom, but this is far from a satisfying outcome.

The women of Unseen University — which is to say, the women of the household staff — are glimpsed here and there throughout the Discworld series, presided over by the mighty Mrs Whitlow. While Mrs Whitlow generally serves as gatekeeper of the rules of the University, on rare occasions she represents disruptive female sexual energy, such as when Music with Rocks In invades the Discworld and she goes full fangirl, up to and including throwing her undergarments at the stage.[14]

In *Unseen Academicals*, the daily life of UU is described as being "as masculine as the smell of old socks and pipe smoke and, given the faculty's general laxness when it came to knocking out their pipes, the smell of smoking socks as well." We learn that Mrs Whitlow specifically chooses her female staff members to be rosy-cheeked, domestic and unsexy — Juliet Stollop being the exception that proved the rule.[15]

The powerful effect of the Unseen University as Masculine Space is further explored in *The Last Continent*, where a group of the faculty (and by accident, Mrs Whitlow) are transported to a surprise magical desert island adventure. Freed of the usual strictures of the university, the wizards experience rapid emotional and social changes, including surprising urges to compete for the attention of Mrs Whitlow, the only woman of the party.[16] The Senior Wrangler is especially affected by Mrs Whitlow's allure.

Later in the same book, the faculty are briefly de-aged. Mrs Whitlow's transformation into an attractive and sensual young woman causes a shock reawakening of several libidos, giving the already-compromised Senior Wrangler a meltdown at the sight of her coconuts.

Just how sexy are wizards anyway?

Despite the overall campaign to convince wizards that sex and magic can't exist in the same place, sex magic does technically exist in the Discworld.

> Ge Fordge's Compenydyum of Sex Majick is kept in a vat of ice in a room all by itself and there's a strict rule that it can only be read by

wizards who are over eighty and, if possible, dead. (*Sourcery*)

The joke is that only old wizards, their sex drive flattened by decades of being surrounded by other old wizards, may apparently study sexual magic as a theory-based subject, as it should be no particular danger to them. A conflation of asexuality with old age is an easy target for humour, though it turns out that age does not (shocker!) preclude sexual interest, least of all in wizards – in fact, when it comes to Discworld wizards and sex (or at least sexual thoughts) we are provided with far more examples among the elderly.

In *Moving Pictures*, a rebellious night out for the Dean, the Chair, The Lecturer in Recent Runes, Windle Poons (the oldest living wizard) and other senior faculty provides the faculty with a startling sexual awakening, thanks to the very attractive Holy Wood star Delores De Syn (Ginger).

Windle Poons has attained a pure state of 'no fucks left to give,' using his advanced age as an excuse to indulge in all manner of activities that other wizards consider undignified or selfish. Unsurprisingly, he is the only wizard who allows himself to enjoy the kick to his libido provided by the glamorous Ginger, while his peers merely find it awkward and confusing... they certainly can't understand why Victor, a former wizarding student, finds it more rewarding to spend his time kissing young ladies for the Clicks than learning to be a wizard.

Later, during their desert island experience in *The Last Continent*, the wizarding faculty are so embarrassed by the very notion of sex that it falls to Mrs Whitlow (previously seen as the bastion of prudery) to enlighten the confused

God of Evolution on the subject of human reproduction -- which she does with surprising gusto and good humour.

In *Unseen Academicals*, the wizards experience romantic stirrings, thanks to the hiring of beauty Juliet Stollop in the Night Kitchen.

Here we are told that wizards practice celibacy "in theory because women were distracting and bad for the magical organs," another explanation that avoids all reference to sourcery (or, indeed, Sourcery).

Juliet's beauty has a profound impact on the wizards. Unlike with Ginger in *Moving Pictures* and Mrs Whitlow in *The Last Continent*, where there was at least a hint of smuttiness among the thoughts of the elderly faculty members, here they process their attraction largely through a lens of innocence: longing looks, daydreams and the quiet urge (never acted upon) to write poetry or buy flowers.[17]

In all these examples where the joke is about elderly celibate men suddenly getting a flutter of sexual or romantic interest in ladies, Ponder Stibbons is left out of the fun. Ponder (the youngest wizard we spend any time with) is written as the most asexual of all wizards in the Discworld, generally responding to the antics of his elder co-workers with a mixture of embarrassment and being-too-busy-to-care.

Unseen Academicals includes several more gems to enlighten us on the sexuality or lack thereof of wizards — such as the Chair of Indefinite Studies' earnest concern that the new football uniform should not include overly short trousers as "it is a well-known fact that a glimpse of the male knee can drive women into a frenzy of libidinousness." It also has to be pointed out to Ridcully by Glenda Sugarbean that the classic uniform design with two Us in front is going to look like comedy boobs; neither he nor the rest of the wizards would have noticed this on their own.

The book also includes a character who shakes up everything we know about Discworld wizards: Professor Bengo Macarona from Genua, where the rule about celibacy is largely ignored. Professor Macarona is not only attractive and excellent at football, he also inspires a significant (and long-overdue) discussion on homosexuality among wizards of the Discworld.

Ponder is reluctant at first to explain to Ridcully about Professor Macarona's past affair with a man; the younger wizard visibly braces himself for Ridcully to say something tremendously offensive in response.[18] Instead, Ridcully cites several other examples of gay wizards he has known and launches into a remarkably sweet speech about acceptance:

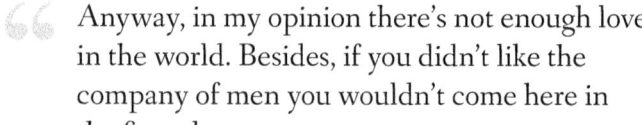

> Anyway, in my opinion there's not enough love in the world. Besides, if you didn't like the company of men you wouldn't come here in the first place.

The 'no sex' rule, clearly, is one that was all about heterosexuality all along, whether to keep ladies away from UU, or to keep sourcery at bay.

Sourcery and Ipslore the Red notwithstanding, the celibacy imposed upon wizards at Unseen University — whether a rule or a guideline — does little to hold them back. In most cases, it is a life choice they appear to have embraced with great enthusiasm, or at least accepted as an easy sacrifice.

The greatest problem stemming from the celibacy rule – and it's clearly not something that the wizards themselves see as a problem – is their isolation from the female half of the population. However, we do see some of the wizards — Ridcully in particular — question whether wizards do in fact have things to learn from women, whether that be Granny Weatherwax or Glenda Sugarbean. Is it possible that, had the Discworld series not lost their author so soon, rumblings of gender equality might finally have shaken Unseen University to its core?

Or, like Professor Tolkien and his friends, were the wizards of Unseen University always to continue largely unchanged in their life of pipe smoke and generous pies, isolated but content?

Tansy Rayner Roberts is a Doctor of Classics, a Doctor Who podcaster, and an author of many science fiction and fantasy books, as well as the essay collection Pratchett's Women. *You can find her at tansyrr.com.*

---

1. It is not acknowledged by the author until very late in the day that there are options other than heterosexual sex and romance.
2. Magic, that is.
3. This discounts the body of women included in the housekeeping and cooking staff, who work hard to make the lives of these bachelor wizards inexpressibly comfortable.
4. Wizards would, incidentally, also prefer the university to be entirely free of students, but they can't have it all their own way.
5. It's not specified whether or not Rincewind's sexual experience with other people pre-dates his wizarding career, or if there is any overlap,

but it is clear that the lack of magic in his life has caused him far more angst.
6. In *Interesting Times*, we are once again shown that sexy women aren't at the top of Rincewind's list of priorities, as his time isolated in the desert only leaves him craving potatoes.
7. This raises more questions than it answers, particularly whether all wizards are literally eighth sons of eighth sons. If so, how on earth are there so many of them?
8. If witches were capable of producing sourcerors, then the fecund line of Nanny Ogg and her forebears would surely have destroyed the world.
9. It seems unlikely that any version of Granny would have allowed things to progress that far; hopefully her knowledge of herbs would have kept their family to a safe size.
10. This is not unique to Unseen University - even Bugurup University in FourEcks had a sign saying *Nulli Sheilae sanguinae*.
11. https://tolkiengateway.net/wiki/User:Ardamir/Essays/Entwives.
12. Of all the questions I wish I had asked Terry Pratchett while I had the chance, "did you base Unseen University on the Inklings and/or the Ents" is now top of the list. If nothing else, it might have made him laugh.
13. I'm not sure if this would have been much consolation from Edith Tolkien's perspective.
14. In *Soul Music*.
15. Glenda Sugarbean, a young woman projecting serious grandma energy, is the perfect example of Mrs Whitlow's hiring policy. Though as it turns out, she does just fine in the attracting chaps department, and not just because of her pies.
16. The role of Mrs Whitlow, Only Woman in the World, as an object of saucy attraction is cemented when she takes her corsets off and develops her own line of full figured beachwear.
17. I think we can all be relieved that things didn't develop in the direction of sexual harassment. Indeed, Juliet remains blissfully unaware of her effect on men in general, and the wizards in particular.
18. Ponder shows remarkable awareness here (for a wizard) of social nuance — he seems especially invested in Ridcully's response to learning of Macarona's sexuality, and attempts to inform him further about the possibility of gay students at UU.

6

FORENSICS FOR FAIRYTALES
MAGIC OR SCIENCE IN SPECULATIVE DETECTIVE FICTION

VJ KNIPE

MURDER IS the most dramatic of crimes. The sudden, forced drop from life into death is both terrifying and intriguing. In her book *A Very British Murder*, Lucy Worsley tells us that the British public has enjoyed reading about real-life murders since the beginning of the nineteenth century. Sir Arthur Conan Doyle capitalised on this interest by creating the most famous literary detective. When first introducing Sherlock Holmes, in *A Study in Scarlet*, the Great Detective is dashing around perfecting a new type of analysis for blood.[1] This is how he works: seek out evidence, analyse it, and use the result to form a conclusion. To the readers of the time this deduction appeared to be magic, but it was pure science.

Since the nineteenth century, mystery stories have evolved. Speculative fiction, both fantasy and science fiction, was a quick adopter of the hunt for clues. As one example, in the 1960s and 1970s, Randall Garrett created his Sherlock-adjacent detective, Lord Darcy. Set in an alternative history, Lord Darcy's world diverges from ours when King Richard the Lionhearted is not killed at the *Siege of Châlus*, as he was in our world, but recovers from his crossbow wound to wisely rule England and France for the rest of his life. During this time the Laws of Magic were codified by St Hilary Robert, a monk at the monastery of Walsingham. Fast forward to the fictional 1960s and 70s and Master Sorcerer Sean O'Lochlainn serves as a Forensic Sorcerer to the Duke of Normandy, working with the investigator, Lord Darcy, using forensic magic to solve crimes.

On the other end of the scale from magic to science, are JD Robb's *In Death* series (1995-ongoing), a set of near-future, science fiction detective novels. Set some thirty years after the Urban Wars of the 2020s, the action takes place in New York City. In this future, prostitution is licensed, with health checks and taxes, and there are sensible gun control laws. A number of the earlier books have Lieutenant Dallas, the NYPD investigator for the series, hunting people who wish to repeal these laws and return to the world prior to the Urban Wars. Throughout all of her In Death novels, JD Robb makes full use of forensics. In later books, for example *Obsession in Death,* the criminal's knowledge of forensic science subverts the evidence. Even so, Dallas relies on forensics to provide the key to the murders.

Both of these book series provide examples at the extreme ends of speculative forensics, one using pure magic and the other pure science, which guide the detective in their hunt for the murderer, and they provided me with comparisons when studying other speculative police fiction. Do the other speculative fiction detectives follow the guidelines laid down by Sherlock Holmes? Forensic Science or Forensic Magic, let's find some clues to solve crime.

A SEARCH through any bookstore will probably provide examples of speculative police procedurals other than those already mentioned. One such is the Inspector Chen novel, *Snake Agent*, by Liz Williams. In *Snake Agent,* even Hell has a police force – to ensure crimes are committed. It is difficult to define the actual genre of *Snake Agent* as Chinese lived beliefs intertwine with modern technology. In my opinion, the nearest genre for *Snake Agent* is urban fantasy. Generally, urban fantasy is set in what we would think of as Our World, but the magic and/or surreal elements are hidden from normal people.[2]

The story starts with a distraught mother afraid that her daughter's ghost has not entered heaven, despite the correct rituals. Following that trail, Inspector Chen discovers that the Imperial Hierarchy of Hell has discovered a way to use the blood and souls of innocent young women to create a pathway to Heaven. Only the human Chen stands in their way, and he has lost the backing of his patron deity because he fell in love with a demon.

Does *Snake Agent* use forensics? Searching the book for keywords associated with forensics brings up 132 references. Colour-coding them provides an interesting pattern (see Appendix for words indexed, and further specifics). 75% of the indicator words came out as 'description'. For instance, using 'blood' as a search word, you find that all demons are described as having 'eyes like drops of blood'. Other findings show that 11% of references refer to magic, 3% to forensic science, and only 1% to forensic magic. At first glance, it appears forensics is not important here.

Despite that, reading through the book indicates a forensics presence:

> 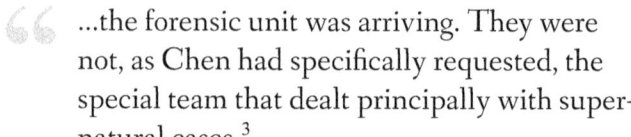...the forensic unit was arriving. They were not, as Chen had specifically requested, the special team that dealt principally with supernatural cases.[3]

This absence requires Inspector Chen to brief the crime scene manager on the *special tests* he needs. Unfortunately, the tests are carried out off-page. By comparison, in the Lord Darcy stories, the Forensic Sorcerer performs the tests on the page, and in the In Death books the detective visits the forensic laboratory to receive results.

Despite this lack, an interesting find in *Snake Agent* is the ghost-tracker, a small lobster-like demon that acts like a cadaver dog.[4] It uses a piece of the ghost's essence to track its prey.

> 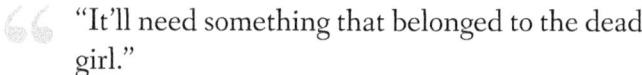"It'll need something that belonged to the dead girl."
>
> "The only thing I've got is a spectral scarf," Chen said, as Lao shuffled from the room. "It'll have to do."[5]

Similarly, in the Lord Darcy series, there is mention of a human 'psychic tracker':

> 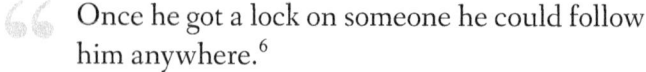Once he got a lock on someone he could follow him anywhere.[6]

And it is not just magic that locates people; in *Concealed in Death* the forensic search team uses a form of electronic 'nose' to locate bodies hidden in the walls.[7] Williams' supernatural sniffer 'dog' has parallels in both magic and science.

Locating the ghost does help Inspector Chen learn that the Hierarchy of Hell is involved, but not the full reason the ghost is lost to heaven. Assisted by Seneschal Zhu Irzh, from the Vice Division of Hell's police force, Chen prevents the Ministry of Epidemics from loosing a plague into Singapore Three, to harvest the innocent souls and blood it requires to carve its stairway to heaven. *Snake Agent* provides a surface dressing of forensics to colour in the scene of police work.

Another urban fantasy police procedural is *Rivers of London* by Ben Aaronvich. *Rivers of London* fits the definition of urban fantasy from The Encyclopedia of Science Fiction (SFE) as if it were the standard model used by the editors.

In this novel, young, biracial Metropolitan police constable, Peter Grant, is exposed to the supernatural world as magic starts to increase after a long period of dwindling. His beat contains not only the unaware humans in London but also the folk of the magical 'Demi-Monde'. In *Rivers of London*, Grant is forced to pit his limited knowledge of magic against the poltergeist spirit of Riot and Rebellion, Mr Punch – as in the Punch and Judy shows. With the help of the Goddess of Beverley Brook and the fae housekeeper of the magic police station, he manages, just, to defeat the spirit, but not before it destroys his closest friend in the Met police force.

Are forensics used in *Rivers of London*? Looking at the analysis, there are 247 sentences in the book that match the search markers. Overall, 53% of those sentences are description, 14% are forensic science, and 3% are forensic magic. Using only words relating to 'blood', we find that 24% is expletive, a pattern not seen in the other books, but remaining consistent with British vernacular.

What *Rivers of London* does have is 'vestigium'. To describe it properly one must return to regular crime scene analysis. The most important thing to remember when dealing with forensic science is Locard's Principle: "Every contact leaves a trace."[8] Once a crime scene is secured, the first thing a Crime Scene Manager or the Senior Investigating Officer does is an initial walk-through. This provides an impression of where the evidence is placed and how it relates to the crime. For the In Death series, Lieutenant Dallas is always shown performing a walk-through, and often marks specific evidence she wants analysed.[9]

Returning to vestigium, magic leaves an impression on a crime scene, in the same way physical evidence does. With training, an investigator can recognise the signs.

Growling, barking, yelling, flashes of cobbles, sticks, laughing – maniacal, high-pitched laughing. I stood up sharply.

'Violence and laughter?' asked Nightingale.

I nodded. 'What was that?' I asked.

'The uncanny,' said Nightingale. 'It's like a bright light when you close your eyes, it leaves an afterimage. We call it vestigium.'

'How do I know I didn't just imagine it?' I asked.

'Experience,' said Nightingale. 'You learn to distinguish the difference through experience.'[10]

This vestigium has a direct link to the Lord Darcy books. Forensic Sorcerer, Master Sean, uses an ankh to focus these magical influences at a crime scene.

> ...your true cross would tend to dissipate the evil. The ankh merely vibrates to evil because of the closed loop at the top, which makes a return circuit.[11]

Despite all the magic and forensic magic in *Rivers of London*, the plot turns on a piece of forensic science, specifically CCTV evidence. PC Grant himself observes that:

> Criminals are not caught by brilliant deductive reasoning but by the fact that some poor slob has spent a week tracking down every shop in Hackney that sells a particular brand of trainer, and then checking the security camera footage on every single one.[12]

Rivers of London bases deductive reasoning on evidence, very much like Sherlock Holmes. In this book, we receive a more in-depth use of forensics than in *Snake Agent*.

Changing over to alternative history[13] we find *A Master of Djinn* by P. Djèlí Clark. This book is a sequel to the novella *A Dead Djinn in Cairo*. Forty years before the series opens, the mystic Al-Jahiz created a Portal to the World called the Kaf, using a magical machine. Through this door, Djinn poured into our world,[14] making Egypt a superpower and placing it far in advance of European attempts at magic. In P. Djèlí Clark's Cairene universe, a supernatural intrusion created an alternate history.

In the books, Agent Fatma el-Sha'arawi is a special investigator with the Egyptian Ministry of Alchemy, Enchantments, and Supernatural Entities. In the initial novella, she shuts down a mechanism called the World Clock just before it destroys everything. The Ministry shut the clock away in their evidence locker guarded by a powerful Djinn. In *A Master of Djinn,* the World Clock is stolen by a person who owns a ring that controls Djinn, including the one guarding the evidence locker. Agent Fatma is required to save the world again. It is in this book that the Department of Supernatural Forensics is introduced.

There has to be forensics in *A Master of Djinn*. An analysis of the search words in *A Master of Djinn* brings up 84 sentences, with 86% as description. But here, unlike the other two books, the forensics are reversed. The mentions are 2% forensic science and 10% forensic magic. When studying the blood-only results, description forms 98% of the markers. Many are derogatory references made by evil djinn about 'half-bloods', offspring of a human-djinn pairing.

Even though the ordinary markers reveal little, forensics are vital to the story. During a fight, Agent Fatma rips a lock of golden (real gold thread) hair from her suspect. Analysis by Supernatural Forensics reveals a spell on the hair that primes people to see what they expect. Thinking that she has broken the spell, Agent Fatma sees black hair, truly believing the perpetrator to be Egyptian.

Hair is one of the important types of forensic evidence. With *Obsession in Death*, the perpetrator is so familiar with evidence collection at crime scenes that nothing can be found:

"Harvo went over to the scene herself 'cause she got it in her head maybe the sweepers missed a hair, a fiber.[15]

Hair and fibre evidence is analysed in similar ways, even in forensic sorcery. In the Lord Darcy series, a scrap of green cloth is reconstituted into a cloak.

> The damaged edges of the cloth will try to find a bit of floc that is most nearly identical to the one that was there previously.[16]

Back in *A Master of Djinn*, Agent Fatma realises that she had expected to see black hair. Understanding this, she manages to break the illusion spell properly.

> Fatma looked to the lock in her hand, and finally, emptied her thoughts. Free of expectations and wants, letting it simply be. The gold coloring of the strands vanished leaving behind a familiar dark red.[17]

This forensic evidence leads Agent Fatma to confront the European culprit. Both the Djinn-controlling ring and the World Clock are destroyed in the conflict. While Agent Fatma does use logic and reasoning, in *A Master of Djinn* she follows the rules laid down by Sherlock Holmes to base her deduction on pure evidence.

So far we've just been looking at the more earnest type of speculative police fiction, but cosy speculative police novels also use forensics. In *Trouble Brewing in Harrogate* by Kim M. Watt, DI Adams investigates tampered beer which causes ordinary, non-magical humans to gain superpowers. When the regular police lab returns negative results, she resorts to consulting a Hedge Witch and a magical talking cat (yes, she requests a cat scan) to annul the magical contamination.

The three main books I have looked at here employ different approaches to the use of forensics, and I enjoyed all of them. Of the three, *Snake Agent* used forensics the least. It was mentioned in passing as something a police procedural should have. But *Snake Agent* was less about finding the murderer, and more about pro-active, anti-terrorist work. Rather than finding the murderer, the detectives, both human and hell-born, had to prevent a mass murder. With my background in Forensic Science, I would have liked a little more evidence, but it barely detracted from the story. In the other two books, the plot turns on forensic evidence, and each time one vital clue leads the detectives to the solution. In a genre that relies on fantasy, that little bit of reality makes the police work more believable. After all, who would believe Sherlock Holmes's deductive reasoning without his measurements of footprints or analysis of blood?

Bibliography

Aaronovitch, Ben. *Rivers of London* (A Rivers of London novel). Orion. Kindle Edition.

Clark, P. Djèlí. *A Master of Djinn*. Little, Brown Book Group. Kindle Edition.

Clute, John, and David Langford. *The Encyclopedia of Science Fiction*. Eds. John Clute and John Grant. Orbit, 1997.

Garrett, Randall. *Lord Darcy* (FANTASY MASTERWORKS). Orion. Kindle Edition.

GFJC. (2013) Principles of Trace Evidence. *A Simplified Guide to Crime Scene Investigation*. Global Forensic and Justice Center. September. https://www.forensicsciencesimplified.org/trace/principles.html

Robb, J. D. *Concealed in Death*. Little, Brown Book Group. Kindle Edition.

Robb, J. D. *Obsession in Death*. Little, Brown Book Group. Kindle Edition.

Watt, Kim M. *Trouble Brewing in Harrogate: A DI Adams mystery - magic, menace, & snark in a Yorkshire urban fantasy* (Book Two). Kim M. Watt. Kindle Edition.

Williams, Liz. *The Detective Inspector Chen Novels Volume One: Snake Agent, The Demon and the City, and Precious Dragon*. Open Road Media. Kindle Edition.

Worsley, Lucy. *A Very British Murder*. Ebury Publishing. Kindle Edition.

Appendix: How did you get those numbers?

My current personal research is studying Speculative Fiction Police Procedurals to see if I can find any Forensics used by the main detective to help solve the crime. I chose to use a modified Braun and Clarke form of thematic analysis.[18] Using the series of search words for forensic ideas, shown in Figure 1, *Rivers of London* produced

Figure 1

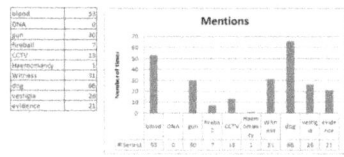

247 sentences that matched the search terms.

I collected the resulting list of search results into Excel and then colour-coded them according to the themes shown in the key, Figure 2.

Figure 2

FORENSICS FOR FAIRYTALES

Description	131
Forensic Science	34
Forensic magic	7
vampires	2
magic	14
haemomancy	8
vestigium	20
sniffer dog	7
expletive	16
car	2
Policing	6

Once coded, the list is sorted into blocks of colour, Figure 3. This gives me numbers for each of the themes.

Figure 3

Putting the numbers into a pie chart, Figure 4, gives me the percentages.

Figure 4

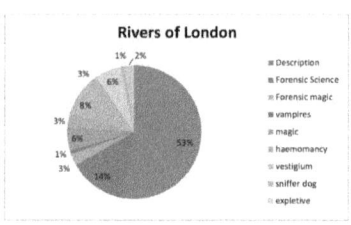

This is, of course, highly simplified. If you want to know more about my workings, I'm happy to go into more detail.

ARMED WITH A BSc BIOCHEMISTRY, an MSc Forensic Science, and a thirst for knowledge, Malaysian-born, Scottish writer, VJ Knipe navigates the realm of fantasy with a touch of the uncanny in a handful of published fantasy books and foray into self-publishing. An avid canoeist, cake decorator, and DIY enthusiast, she's also a passionate advocate for autism awareness. Her current work-in-progress is a police procedural set on Mars and she has a long-running, monthly forensic science article for an online magazine.

---

1. Initially the test for blood required a liquid state and was identified under a microscope. A new test which turned blue in the presence of blood (dried or otherwise) arrived in 1862. As *A Study in Scarlet* was written in 1887, this chemical test might be the one Holmes is 'perfecting'.
2. About now, I should point out that I take my definitions from SFE, The Encyclopedia of Science Fiction.
    "Urban Fantasies are normally texts where fantasy and the mundane world intersect and interweave throughout a tale which is significantly about a real city." https://sf-encyclopedia.com/fe/urban_fantasy Clute, John, and David Langford. "Urban Fantasy." *The Encyclopedia of Science Fiction*. Eds. John Clute and John

Grant. Orbit, 1997. Web. 16 Oct. 2024. <sf-encyclopedia.com/fe/urban_fantasy>.
3. Williams, p38.
4. Cadaver dogs are specialist detection dogs trained from a puppy to search out human remains. They distinguish between human and animal remains. Their noses detect a corpse over 3 metres underground or even underwater.
5. Williams, p.110.
6. Garrett, p.485.
7. Robb, *Concealed in Death*, p.7.
8. GFJC, 2013.
9. Robb, *Obsession in Death*, p.208.
10. Aaronovitch, p.38.
11. Garrett, p.15.
12. Aaronovitch, p.64.
13. So that we are all on the same page, Alternate History according to SFE is: *"An account of Earth (sometimes extending to exploration of solar-system space) as it might have become in consequence of some hypothetical alteration in history."* Stableford, Brian M, Gary K Wolfe and David Langford. "Alternate History." *The Encyclopedia of Science Fiction*. Eds. John Clute and David Langford. SFE Ltd/Ansible Editions, 25 Jan. 2021. Web. 16 June 2023. <https://sf-encyclopedia.com/entry/alternate_history>.
14. Making this also an Intrusion Fantasy, a story "which features supernatural intrusions into our own world Nicholls, Peter. "Fantasy." The Encyclopedia of Science Fiction. Eds. John Clute and David Langford. Ansible Editions, 3 July 2023. Web. 16 Oct. 2024. <sf-encyclopedia.com/entry/fantasy>.
15. Robb, *Obsession in Death*, p.54.
16. Garrett, p.139.
17. Clark, p.328.
18. Virginia Braun, Victoria Clarke, Nikki Hayfield and Gareth Terry. *Thematic Analysis: A Reflective Approach*. [online] available at https://www.psych.auckland.ac.nz/en/about/thematic-analysis.html accessed 04/08/2020

7

WHAT LIES AND THREATS

HISTORY AND NATIONALIST MYTH-MAKING IN THE LORD OF THE RINGS

ABBY ROBERTS

J.R.R. Tolkien was a philologist, not a scholar of myth. He admitted as much in "On Fairy-Stories," an essay originally given as a lecture in 1939. Nonetheless, "On Fairy-Stories" shows Tolkien was knowledgeable about myth scholarship of his and preceding generations and had drawn his own conclusions on the origins and functions of myth. For Tolkien, myth was the process by which human beings comprehend and describe the world around them: "The incarnate mind, the tongue, and the tale are in our world coeval."

Tolkien had begun writing *The Lord of the Rings* at about the time he delivered "On Fairy-Stories." His ideas about the cognitive role of myth play out in the novel. When characters look up at the constellation readers identify as Ursa Major, the Big Dipper, or the Plow, they know it as the Sickle of the godlike Valar. Whether dealing with difficulties or meeting the love of their life, they think of themselves as participants in a chain of events begun long ago by heroes such as the clever Elvish princess Lúthien and her hapless mortal lover Beren. Through these blended mythic-historic narratives, characters imagine their collective pasts and create identity and meaning, as real people do.

In particular, the histories Tolkien created for the fictional kingdoms of Gondor and Rohan, presented in the main text and appendices of *The Lord of the Rings*, resemble mythopoeic narratives created by ancient, medieval, and modern states. Tolkien did not create these histories for the purpose of indulging himself, generating trivia for fans, or providing a rulebook for his setting. These narratives not only provide insights into the beliefs, motivations, and self-conceptions of Tolkien's characters but also comment on the role of myth in real-world societies.

Gondor: A Myth of a Golden Age

A myth is a story that members of a community tell themselves about who they are and where they come from. Myths may create shared meanings that bring people together, although they may also create scapegoats, outcasts, and enemies. Most modern scholarship stresses that myths are not necessarily false, although they are often selective or distorted tellings of the truth. More importantly, myths are believed to be true by their audiences.

As such, myth is easily entangled in history, and a community's origins are a common target for mythopoeia. Greeks and Romans in the ancient Mediterranean credited the founding of their cities to mythic survivors of the Trojan War. The collection of annals known as the *Anglo-Saxon Chronicle* include Woden in the genealogies of historic kings because the once-god's role as an ancestor figure persisted after the people had become Christian. Modern nation-states also mythologize their founders. As an American, I was raised on myths about figures such as George Washington, Thomas Jefferson, and Alexander Hamilton. These foundation myths create models of what communities "should" be like and provide (ostensibly) virtuous examples for members to emulate.

According to the "official history" in Appendix A of *The Lord of the Rings,* the people of Gondor trace their origins to Númenor, an island civilization that was once the heart of a world-spanning empire. When the last Númenorean king invaded the land of the Valar themselves, more than three thousand years before the events of *The Lord of the Rings,* Númenor and most of its people were destroyed. A few survivors, led by Elendil and Isildur, escaped to the Númenorean colonies on the mainland of Middle-earth, where they founded the realm of Gondor. Elendil and Isildur were then instrumental in defeating the Dark Lord Sauron when he first rose to power. In time, Gondor also became a vast empire, powerful on land and sea. So great was its wealth, "precious stones are pebbles in Gondor for children to play with."

This narrative recalls a type of myth common since antiquity—the myth of the "golden age." For Anglophones, golden age myths may include narratives relating to Arthurian Britain, Republican Rome, and Classical Athens. These narratives imagine a past in which the community supposedly attained a pure, authentic state. They may focus on the community's past economic, political, religious, and intellectual achievements.

The myth of Gondor's golden age is important to how Gondorian characters understand themselves and present themselves to others. "Believe not that in the land of Gondor the blood of Númenor is spent, nor all its pride and dignity forgotten," Boromir declares when he introduces himself to Elrond's council. "By our valour the wild folk of the East are still restrained, and the terror of Morgul kept at bay; and thus alone are peace and freedom maintained in the lands behind us, bulwark of the West." He invokes several elements of Gondor's national myth: its Númenorean inheritance, military might, and defiance of Sauron.

However, other characters do not accept this version of history. Aragorn challenges Boromir's claim that Gondor is responsible for the defense of Middle-earth and reminds him that other Númenorean descendants dwell outside the kingdom's borders. "You know little of the lands beyond your bounds," Aragorn says. "What roads would any dare to tread, what safety would there be in quiet lands, or in the homes of simple men at night, if the Dúnedain were asleep, or were all gone into the grave?" Then, Gandalf informs the council that Sauron survived through the actions of Isildur —an event conveniently forgotten in Gondor. This is the first significant indication in the novel that Tolkien's characters narrate the past *as they understand it* and that readers cannot always take them at face value.

Boromir, a man of action, is not prone to reflecting on history, but his brother, Faramir, has a more complicated relationship with Gondor's mythologized past. That he values his country's intellectual achievements is clear in his best-known quotation about loving not the weapons of war but what they defend: "the city of the Men of Númenor," as he calls Gondor's capital of Minas Tirith. "I would have her loved for her memory, her anciency, her beauty, and her present wisdom." Faramir reveres Gondor's Númenorean inheritance, but he notes that many Númenoreans have served Sauron and reflects on the hubris that led to the civilization's downfall.

Aragorn, the Ranger who becomes king, is not Gondorian, but he cannily invokes Gondor's national myth before ascending the throne. He sets out from Rivendell with Elendil's sword reforged and renamed as Andúril, "Flame of the West," to recall the memory of Númenor, the westernmost land inhabited by mortal beings in Tolkien's created geography. In Gondor, Aragorn locates a descendent of a sacred tree that grew in the capital of Númenor and replants it in Minas Tirith. At his coronation, he recites the words spoken by Elendil upon his arrival in Middle-earth. One of Aragorn's regnal names is Envinyatar, "the Renewer" in Tolkien's constructed language of Quenya. Renewal is another significant component of golden age myths—leaders often proclaim their intent to restore to a community the glory it enjoyed in the past.

One result of Aragorn's invocation of Gondor's mythologized past is that he proves his claim to the throne despite his outsider status. Another is that he is able to rally the soldiers of Gondor and their allies to march on the gates of Mordor, offering a battle that he hopes will allow Frodo to destroy the One Ring and save Middle-earth, but which Aragorn himself cannot expect to survive. One of the functions of myth is to motivate members of a community to act collectively, especially in times of hardship. But not all uses of myth are so constructive.

Rohan: A Myth of Territory

While the Gondorians discover their origins in written accounts of Númenor's downfall, the people of Rohan look to songs of their heroic ancestors. About five hundred years before the events of *The Lord of the Rings*, Appendix A relates, a people known as the Éothéod lived in the north of Middle-earth. Their leaders included the dragon-slaying Fram and horse-taming Eorl. When the Éothéod assisted the Gondorian army in battle, the ruling Gondorian steward awarded a northern province to the people. They became known as Rohirrim, and the country, Rohan. There they lived idyllically as "free men under their own kings and laws."

This "official history" asserts the region had been depopulated before the Rohirirm arrived, but—as is often the case with myths like this—this is not true. In fact, the region was already (and is still) inhabited by a people referred to as "Dunlendings," since the Rohirrim then drove many of them into the adjacent territory of Dunland. Tolkien clearly did not forget about the Dunlendings when he wrote Appendix A—he mentions them again only a few pages later. The most logical assumption is that readers are intended to notice the discrepancy.

The Dunlendings get little time on page, but through the character of Gamling, Tolkien indicates in *The Two Towers* that the Dunlendings' collective memory of expulsion was used by Saruman to recruit them for his invasion of Rohan:

[The Dunlendings] hate us, and they are glad; for our doom seems certain to them. 'The king, the king!' they cry. 'We will take the king. Death to the Forgoil! Death to the Strawheads! Death to the robbers of the North!' Such names they have for us. Not in half a thousand years have they forgotten their grievance that the lords of Gondor gave the Mark to Eorl the Young and made alliance with him. That old hatred Saruman has inflamed.

Although Gamling is Rohirric, he claims knowledge of the Dunlending language and views on history. This hints at Gamling having interacted closely with Dunlendings, despite the enmity between the groups.

Appendix A likewise hints at cohabitation between Dunlendings and Rohirrim in an episode that occurred about two hundred and fifty years after the latter's arrival in Rohan. Freca, a nobleman of both Rohirric and Dunlending descent, approaches Helm, king of Rohan, to propose a marriage between Helm's daughter and Freca's son. Helm takes affront at the offer. The exchange decays into petty insults relating to weight and age and Freca's Dunlending ancestry before a fight breaks out, in which Helm kills Freca. Helm then declares Freca's son, Wulf, an outlaw. Wulf flees Rohan but returns four years later with a Dunlending army.

The Dunlendings, and Rohirrim of Dunlending descent such as Freca and Wulf, contest the Rohirrim's "myth of territory." This type of myth sacralizes a given territory as the place where a community attained its ideal state. Often, this land must be safeguarded from anyone the community deems an outsider. Freca considers himself Rohirric enough to propose the union of his family to Helm's, but Helm names Freca a Dunlending, enforcing Freca and Wulf's outsider status before killing one and exiling the other.

Myths may create categories, order them within hierarchies, and naturalize and legitimize discriminatory systems. Analysis of a myth may begin by identifying the categories of people and other beings set out in the narrative, how these categories are ranked, and how the narrative justifies this ranking. In the narrative of Helm and Freca, Tolkien establishes the categories of "person of Rohan" and "Dunlending" and makes clear the Rohirrim believe themselves superior to Dunlendings. Yet these categories are not inborn but enforced by people, such as Helm. Nor are they exclusionary, if Dunlendings and Rohirrim intermarry and learn each other's languages.

Moreover, Tolkien's narrative of the war between the Dunlendings led by Wulf and Rohirrim led by Helm does not portray the latter as a heroic figure. Helm kills Freca in a petty argument and is later revealed to be a cold-blooded murderer: leaving his winter refuge, Helm would "stalk like a snow-troll into the camps of his enemies, and slay many men with his hands," Tolkien writes. "The Dunlendings said that if he could find no food he ate men." The war is not presented as a glorious triumph over savage outsiders but a tragedy, sparked by Helm's pride, that leads to the deaths of Helm, Wulf, Helm's sons, and many others, weakening Rohan for years. Overall, this narrative complicates rather than reinforces the Rohirrim's self-conception as a heroic people who are the rightful rulers of Rohan.

Complicating Created Histories

The incident between Helm and Freca is not the only point where Tolkien subtly undermines his characters' myths of history. Faramir informs Sam and Frodo in *The Two Towers* that the Númenorean aristocracy did not expel the indigenous people of Gondor. However, Gondorian characters express a hostility comparable to Rohirric hatred of Dunlendings toward the peoples of southern realms, especially that of Umbar. The main text and appendices establish that Gondor and Umbar have a long, shared history: Umbar is another former Númenorean colony, it was once a Gondorian colony as well, and the two realms have often been at war with each other.

According to Appendix A, the mutual animosity began about sixteen hundred years before the War of the Ring. Valacar, king of Gondor, marries Vidumavi, a foreign princess who Gondorians consider to be of a "lesser and alien race." In Tolkien's works, Númenoreans often express disdain for non-Númenorean peoples. Númenoreans also believe—wrongly, as Tolkien makes clear—that intermarriage with other peoples reduces the extended lifespans gifted to them by the Valar. When the son of Valacar and Vidumavi, Eldacar, succeeds the throne, rebellion ignites among Gondorian aristocrats who believe his mixed heritage illegitimizes his rule. Eldacar eventually prevails in a civil war that destroys Gondor's former capital, Osgiliath. The rebels flee to Umbar, then under Gondorian rule, where they establish a base to launch further attacks. This conflict continues until the War of the Ring, when Aragorn must summon an army of ghosts to liberate Gondor's southern fiefs from Umbarian occupation.

The relationship between Gondor and Umbar parallels that between the Rohirrim and Dunlendings. As the Dunlendings disrupt the Rohirric territorial myth, Umbar's existence challenges Gondorian myths of Númenorean inheritance, military might, and defiance of Sauron. Umbarians have as much a claim to the lost empire's legacy as Gondorians, and their military strength is great enough to challenge Gondor's. That Umbar aligns with Sauron despite sharing much of its history and culture with Gondor implies the latter may just as easily fall under the Dark Lord's sway. Umbar challenges Gondorian self-image just as the Dunlendings that of the Rohirrim.

For all the high fantasy trappings of Tolkien's novel, he went to great lengths to establish that the primary historic enemies of Gondor and Rohan were not monstrous or supernatural entities but *human* societies made up of outcasts from both kingdoms. Moreover, with much less effort, he could have constructed narratives that confirmed rather than challenged Rohirric and Gondorian national myths and upheld both states as straightforwardly heroic. That he complicated his created histories as he did indicates he was making a thematic point.

Tolkien and Nationalist Myth

The significance of Tolkien's created histories is not that they present "facts" about societies that never existed but that they speak to human behavior in the real world. In the two major state societies depicted in *The Lord of the Rings*, myth functions like it does in modern nation-states.

Rohirrim and Gondorians tell myths founded in history that help them understand their places in the world, consolidate political power, and band together in times of difficulty. Revealingly, both kingdoms also wage self-destructive wars against outsiders whose difference is established not by inborn traits but by these same myths. Tolkien created a setting in which nationalist myth-making leads directly to violence. Through implication, he suggests the same is true in the readers' world.

Admittedly, the extent to which Tolkien expects readers to agree or disagree with his characters' beliefs and prejudices is often unclear. Characters' descriptions of "wild men of the East" and "cruel Haradrim" go mostly unchallenged by the narrative, and readers should not explain the racism in Tolkien's works as emanating solely from his characters' subjective points of view. However, Tolkien's novel supports multiple, even contradictory meanings. His created histories are too carefully developed for the implications about the dangers of nationalist myth to be accidents of runaway worldbuilding.

Although Tolkien never sought to create a "mythology for England," as fans and critics sometimes claim, literary scholar Dimitra Fimi identifies nationalistic motivations in Tolkien's early writings. In her book *Tolkien, Race and Cultural History,* Fimi tracks how these influences diminished over Tolkien's lifetime, beginning at about the time of *The Hobbit*'s publication in 1937. When *The Lord of the Rings* was published in 1954–55, Tolkien "knew much more about nation formation and about how peoples, languages and traditions intermingle," Fimi writes. "Courtesy of World War II he also had an acute awareness of the dangers of insisting on 'racial' or even just national purity;

he knew how origin and cultural myths could be misused and appropriated." Ultimately, in the last two decades of his life, Tolkien became increasingly critical of the mythopoeic elements in his work, which Fimi argues contributed to his failure to complete *The Silmarillion*. Tolkien's self-reflection mirrors the general soul-searching that occurred among postwar myth scholars, as they reckoned with their discipline's role in the Holocaust and World War II.

When Tolkien wrote *The Lord of the Rings,* he had not yet lost his taste for mythopoeia, but a clear invitation for readers to reflect on nationalist myth-making appears in *The Two Towers,* when Sam sees the body of a Haradian soldier killed by Gondorian Rangers. Although he has just heard two Rangers curse the Haradrim as allies of Sauron, his thoughts go out to the dead man:

It was Sam's first view of a battle of Men against Men, and he did not like it much. He was glad that he could not see the dead face. He wondered what the man's name was and where he came from; and if he was really evil of heart, or what lies or threats had led him on the long march from his home; and if he would not really rather have stayed there in peace—all in a flash of thought which was quickly driven from his mind.

Sam ponders not only the man's identity but the narratives —"lies or threats"—that had motivated him to kill strangers in a foreign land. This recalls the Dunlendings' "old hatred" exploited by Saruman, which is not a lie in the sense of being a total fabrication but *is* a selective telling of the truth that ignores past coexistence with the Rohirrim. It also recalls Rohirric and Gondorian hatred for "wild hill-men" and "cursed Southrons" and the half-truths they tell themselves, erasing more complicated histories. In Middle-earth, violence against outsiders is not only a consequence of nationalist myth-making but directly encouraged by it, a theme that resonates with Tolkien's life experience as a veteran of one world war and witness to another.

Because Tolkien's worldbuilding speaks to historic realities, this passage also calls on readers to consider mythopoeic narratives in their own societies. Not all uses of myth are destructive, but the myths employed by modern nation-states easily enable violence against *someone*. As I write this, the people of the United States have reelected a presidential candidate who has promised violence against "outsiders": immigrants, ethnic and racial minorities, women, and members of the queer and transgender communities. It has been more than a year since the beginning of genocide in Palestine, and more than two years since the invasion of Ukraine. These events did not occur out of spontaneous hatred. They are enabled not only by impersonal societal structures and the malice of individuals but also by narratives people create about the past and their relationships to it.

In this historical moment, we should consider what myths look like, how they are created and transmitted, who they include and exclude, and what other effects they bring about. It's important we assess not only the myths we identify as harmful or that are believed by other people, but also the narratives we draw meaning from ourselves.

Further Reading

Myth Scholarship:

Flood, Christopher G. *Political Myth: A Theoretical Introduction*. New York: Routledge, 2002.

Lincoln, Bruce. *Theorizing Myth: Narrative, Ideology, and Scholarship*. Chicago: University of Chicago Press, 1999.

Schöpflin, George. "The Functions of Myth and a Taxonomy of Myths." In *Myths and Nationhood*, edited by Geoffrey Hocking and George Schöpflin, 19-35. New York: Routledge, 1997.

Smith, Anthony. "'The Golden Age' and National Renewal." In *Myths and Nationhood*, edited by Geoffrey Hocking and George Schöpflin, 36-59. New York: Routledge, 1997.

<u>Tolkien Scholarship:</u>

Bowman, Mary R. "The Story Was Already Written: Narrative Theory in *The Lord of the Rings*." *Narrative* 14, no. 3 (2006). Accessed October 19, 2024. https://www.jstor.org/stable/20107391.

Brown, Sara. "Remembering and Forgetting: National Identity Construction in Tolkien's Middle-earth." *Journal of Tolkien Research* 19, no. 3 (2024). Accessed October 19, 2024. https://scholar.valpo.edu/journaloftolkienresearch/vol19/iss3/8.

Emanuel, Tom. "By the Waters of Anduin We Lay Down and Wept: Tolkien's *Akallabêth* and the Prophetic Imagination." *Mallorn* no. 64 (2023).

Fimi, Dimitra. *Tolkien, Race and Cultural History: From Fairies to Hobbits*. Basingstoke, UK: Palgrave Macmillan, 2010.

<u>Works by J.R.R. Tolkien:</u>

The Fellowship of the Ring, 2nd edition. Boston: Houghton Mifflin Company, 1965.

The Return of the King, 2nd edition. Boston: Houghton Mifflin Company, 1965.

The Two Towers, 2nd edition. Boston: Houghton Mifflin Company, 1965.

"On Fairy-Stories." In *The Monsters and the Critics and Other Essays*, 109-157. London: HarperCollins, 2006.

ABBY ROBERTS IS *a writer of science fiction and fantasy who enjoys medieval history and indie rock. She lives in Virginia, United States, with her dog, Violet.*

8

REIMAGINING DISABILITY IN YA FANTASY

EXPLORING HARPER AND RHEN IN A CURSE SO DARK AND LONELY

EMILIE MORSCHECK

Introduction

THE JOURNEY of the Young Adult (YA) fantasy protagonist is always a physically and emotionally demanding one. Readers expect action and high stakes to carry them through the narrative. The YA protagonist must be competent enough to fulfil these feats, but be flawed enough to be relatable to their teenage audience. Character growth is a necessity for any YA novel, regardless of genre, and it is another expectation that the flaws of the character will be eliminated or reduced by the end of the journey.

The character of the YA protagonist archetype has begun to change in recent years, particularly with the inception of the #ownvoices movement in 2015, which advocated for works written by authors of marginalised groups writing about their own experiences. While conversations and terminology have changed since 2015, readers' desire to consume diverse content by diverse authors has only grown.[1] The depiction of disability in YA fantasy has evolved and expanded alongside the #ownvoices movement. However, it is still rare to see a permanently disabled protagonist in fiction: Ria Cheyne states that "Disability's associations with dependency, inability, and passivity also threaten to undermine the aspirational, heroic, and achieving ethos of fantasy, misfitting with the genre's affective imperatives."[2] This essay will consider the construction and representation of disability in YA fantasy, with a specific focus on the novel *A Curse So Dark and Lonely* by Brigid Kemmerer (2019). In *A Curse So Dark and Lonely*, Kemmerer reimagines the roles available to disabled characters, through the protagonists of Harper and Rhen.

A Curse So Dark and Lonely is a retelling of Beauty and the Beast in which the protagonist, Harper, ends up in the magical realm of Emberfall and comes to the attention of Prince Rhen. Rhen has been cursed to turn into a monster unless he can find a girl to fall in love with him, and he is also dealing with the collapse of his kingdom. Harper appears to be his only hope for breaking the curse, but she is only concerned with surviving and returning home to the real world where her family needs her. The novel follows the pair as they face challenges and fall in love. The narrative of *A Curse So Dark and Lonely* is typical YA fantasy fare, with light politics, action, adventure, and a romance. However, Kemmerer begins with a subversion of expectations through the character of Harper. Harper has Cerebral Palsy (CP), making her anything but the typical YA protagonist. Rather than being a complete departure from the norm, Harper represents an evolution of the YA protagonist archetype, blending familiar traits with new dimensions of resilience and authenticity.

Theoretical Framework

Inclusion of disabled characters in YA fantasy is challenged by both the pervasiveness of disability metanarratives and the need for accurate, empathetic representation of disability. This section will delve into representation theory and disability theory, examining how these frameworks illuminate the portrayal of disability in YA fantasy.

In contemporary western culture, metanarratives of disability are as persistent as fantasy genre character archetypes such as the hero, the mentor, and the villain. Disability is reduced to tropes, stereotypes and repetitive narratives.[3] Works that include disabled characters often position them in the background of the narrative as secondary or tertiary characters, teaching the protagonist about loss, overcoming adversity, and redemption. Within the realm of fantasy literature, disability metanarratives often intersect with broader cultural ideals of heroism, power, and identity. As Cheyne observes, the genre's emphasis on aspirational and heroic figures can present challenges for the author wanting to include disabled protagonists, as disability is often perceived as antithetical to these ideals.[4] For a protagonist to be disabled, the author is required to acknowledge and confront these prevailing metanarratives, prompting a reconsideration of established norms and inviting readers to engage with disability in more nuanced and authentic ways.

Of course, the metanarratives of disability are not the only challenges to the development of a disabled protagonist. How a disability is represented within the story is just as critical. However, what makes for 'good' representation is not simple to define. Jen Webb notes: "What seems to be true, right or accurate is, generally speaking, only true, right or accurate when it fits with a particular social, historical, and personal perspective".[5] This observation underscores the fluid and subjective nature of perceptions of representation. The criteria for evaluating what constitutes 'good' representation evolves over time and is also culturally subjective. This paper will not be judging the accuracy of CP representation in *A Curse So Dark and Lonely,* but rather examining how the book portrays disability within the narrative.

Before discussing the narrative itself, it is important to consider authorial intent. Within the Author's Note and Acknowledgements, Kemmerer recognises that CP is a disability that is not singular in experience or presentation, that she conducted research into CP, and engaged with individuals with CP to develop Harper. The Author's Note states, "Harper's experience may not be reflective of all people with CP, but hopefully her determination and tenacity will be relatable to everyone," and the Acknowledgement states, "Additional thanks to Claerie Kavanagh for doing an impressively thorough sensitivity read, and offering amazing suggestions for where I could add clarity about Harper's CP and her abilities" (pp. 480–484). Kemmerer's intent in creating a positive representation of CP is clear in her statements.

This paper represents a portion of a larger research project examining the representation of disability in YA fairy tale retellings. The novel was selected from a larger list of titles for its explicit portrayal of a disabled protagonist and clear references to the fairy tale source material. In the following sections, we will explore how Brigid Kemmerer tackles these challenges in *A Curse So Dark and Lonely*, examining the portrayal of Harper and Rhen as the protagonists. Through a critical analysis of the novel, we will uncover the ways in which Kemmerer, a non-disabled author, challenges disability metanarratives, and invites readers to reconsider their perceptions of disability in fantasy literature.

Harper

> I strove to create a girl who was strong, resilient, and capable— not in spite of any physical challenges she might face, but in addition to them. (p. 480)

Harper is the primary protagonist of *A Curse So Dark and Lonely,* playing the role of the Beauty from the Beauty and the Beast narrative. As the beauty of Kemmerer's tale, Harper is expected to persevere and show the beast that he can be loved by falling in love with him.

Her introduction in chapter two gives the reader insight into how she views herself. Harper is placed in the middle of the action, supporting her brother, Jake, while he does the dirty work of a loan shark. The first hint that Harper might be 'different' comes while she reflects on her role: "I'm not quick, and I'm not strong. Playing lookout is the only way he'll let me help." (p. 7). Harper's CP is revealed on the following page:

> Jake would be so pissed. I have one job here. I imagine him yelling. *Don't get involved Harper! You're already vulnerable!* He's right, but cerebral palsy doesn't mean my curiosity is broken. (p. 8)

We learn that Harper has a desire to be useful, and that her brother, Jake, sees her as someone to be protected. As Harper is yet to enter Emberfall, these views are positioned within the narrative to reflect those of the real world. To Jake, and most of the people around her in the real world, Harper is a burden, and lacking in agency; someone to protect.

However, like most YA protagonists, Harper has a strong sense of justice and a willingness to take action, even at a cost to herself. While on lookout, Harper witnesses a young woman about to be kidnapped, and she can't help but intervene. Her quick action saves the woman, but Harper is captured instead. She is therefore transported by magic to Emberfall, and brought to the castle of Prince Rhen. In Emberfall, the world she knows is gone. Emberfall is a world of poverty, war, and magic. While gender roles are somewhat flexible—women can take on jobs such as being a soldier and rulers without controversy—they still reflect the traditional hierarchies and expectations of a pseudo-medieval society. Disability in the world of Emberfall is often the result of injury. Rhen's first impression of Harper is that she has been injured: "I wonder if Grey has injured her, the way she keeps the weight off her left leg" (p. 11). Harper, terrified of being kidnapped, takes advantage of Rhen's assumption that she is weakened, attacking him and attempting to run away. While Harper doesn't get far, as there is no way she can escape the magical world on her own, this further reveals her character: she is a survivor, and unwilling to give up. Her disability forces her to come up with alternate solutions to challenges; knowing she can't run far or fast, she seeks out a horse. And Harper knows how to use the element of surprise to get the best of an attacker.

She also knows when her physical limitations are going to hold her back from the obvious path forward. Harper is soon caught by Prince Rhen and his commander Grey, and they return her to the castle. Harper's first impressions of the two men are as attackers, but in their chase, she recognises they are not the villains she is used to in the real world:

> 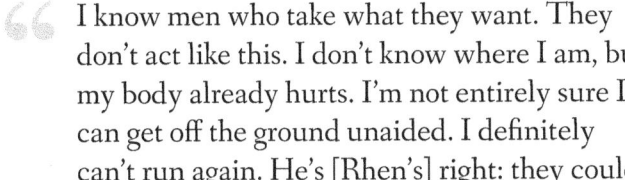 I know men who take what they want. They don't act like this. I don't know where I am, but my body already hurts. I'm not entirely sure I can get off the ground unaided. I definitely can't run again. He's [Rhen's] right: they could take me by force. I should conserve my energy. I can rest. I can eat. I'll find a way out. (p. 23)

Kemmerer's construction of Harper acknowledges the challenges of CP, while maintaining Harper's autonomy in her own story. Harper is never without a plan, even when she is in pain.

Kemmerer challenges the disability metanarrative of the helpless or passive victim of disability through Harper's character. Harper's CP neither defines nor diminishes her. Where a common disability metanarrative is to simplify or tokenise a disabled character, Kemmerer gives Harper the leading role. Through Harper's narrative arc, readers witness her struggles, triumphs, and moments of vulnerability, gaining insight into the intricacies of her lived experience. Kemmerer's research was conducted to ensure that her representation of CP in the novel was grounded in authenticity and nuance. While Harper serves as a rebuttal of prevailing disability narratives, she fits many of the stereotypes of a YA protagonist. She has strength, resilience, and agency. Through this, Kemmerer demonstrates that there truly needn't be much that separates a non-disabled protagonist from a disabled one in YA, and that there is no reason to exclude disabled characters from leading roles. Ultimately, Harper isn't a reinvention of the YA protagonist, but an evolution of one.

Rhen

As *A Curse So Dark and Lonely* is a retelling of Beauty and the Beast, Rhen fulfils the role of the beast to be saved through the love of Harper. As the cursed prince of Emberfall, Rhen grapples with the physical and emotional ramifications of his condition, struggling to reconcile his monstrous form with his sense of self-worth and humanity. After his first transformation into the monster, Rhen goes on a murderous rampage, killing everyone in the castle, including his family. Despite his initial reluctance to confront his curse, with Harper's aid Rhen embarks on a journey of self-discovery and redemption, confronting his own prejudices and reevaluating his understanding of power and agency. Through his interactions with Harper and other characters, Rhen learns to embrace vulnerability as a source of strength rather than weakness. Kemmerer has developed this character arc to complement and contrast with Harper's.

Rhen's self-introduction offers a glimpse into the inner turmoil that shapes his character. From the outset, fear permeates his thoughts, underscoring the weight of his curse and the atrocities it compels him to commit. Rhen tells the reader, "There is blood under my fingernails. I wonder how many of my people I've killed this time" (p. 1). As the first line of the novel, the reader is given key information to Rhen's understanding of himself. He sees himself as an unredeemable monster, a killer.

His introduction contrasts with Harper's in a striking way. Where it takes a few pages to mention her CP, Rhen's narration tells the reader what he thinks of himself from the first line. Rhen's self-perception serves to highlight Harper's sense of agency. Both are in situations that they can't control, but only Harper initially has the perseverance to fight for her goals and beliefs. While Rhen initially conforms to the archetype of the standard love interest, it becomes evident that his role extends beyond mere romantic entanglement. As the narrative unfolds, Rhen's character undergoes a transformation that challenges preconceived notions about power, agency, and identity. While Harper remains the focal point of the story, Rhen's presence serves to complement and enrich her journey, rather than overshadow it.

In the realm of YA fantasy, protagonists often embody a mix of familiar traits: courage, determination, and a sense of duty. Rhen, like Harper, fits into this archetype. At the heart of Rhen's character is a profound sense of duty to his kingdom and its people. Despite his curse and the impending doom it brings, Rhen remains committed to protecting Emberfall and its inhabitants. His actions are driven not only by a desire to break the curse but also by a genuine concern for the welfare of his subjects.

However, fear is a larger motivation for Rhen:

> 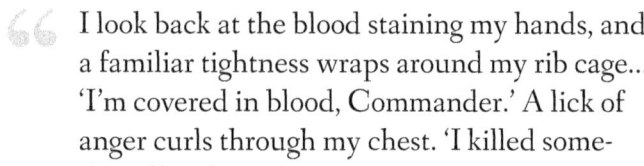 I look back at the blood staining my hands, and a familiar tightness wraps around my rib cage... 'I'm covered in blood, Commander.' A lick of anger curls through my chest. 'I killed something.'(p. 2)

Rhen stays away from his people because he fears turning into a monster and killing them as he killed his family.

In contrast to Harper's journey of physical and emotional resilience, Rhen's arc revolves around vulnerability and self-discovery. While Harper grapples with the harsh realities of Emberfall, learning to navigate its dangers and overcome its obstacles, Rhen confronts his own inner demons, gradually shedding the layers of self-doubt and mistrust that have long defined him. Towards the middle of the novel, Rhen opens up to Harper about his family and the fact that he killed them while he was the monster: "We're face to face. Her cheeks are reddened and her eyes damp. My own tears don't feel far off" (pp. 186–187). As Harper grows stronger, Rhen learns to embrace his own vulnerability, opening himself up to the possibility of love and redemption.

Kemmerer's depiction of Rhen's curse may not have been intended as a commentary on disability representation, yet it nevertheless contributes to the ongoing discussion surrounding metanarratives of disability in literature.

Cheyne notes, "disability is frequently linked with magic in the genre: either disabled people have privileged access to magic, or disability is cured or created by magical means."[6] In many fantasy narratives, disability is often represented as an irreversible condition that reflects moral or personal failure, or it is cured through magical means. Despite the parallels between Rhen's curse and traditional representations of disability in fantasy literature, it's important to note that his condition is distinct from physical or cognitive impairments. Kemmerer's portrayal of Rhen's curse does challenge some common disability stereotypes. The curse, which was cast by an evil sorceress for political gain rather than being an inherent "disability," focuses on Rhen's loss of agency rather than a traditional physical or cognitive impairment. This framing shifts the narrative away from the typical disability tropes, such as magical cures or punishments, and towards one of injustice and power manipulation. The narrative centres on Rhen's internal struggle with his identity and his desire to reclaim control over his kingdom, which contrasts with the common trope of disability being used as a tool for personal or moral growth through magical means or a cure. This emphasis on agency, rather than physical limitation, breaks from the traditional stereotype of disability in fantasy literature and opens up new possibilities for how we think about characters who experience suffering or limitation. Rhen tells the reader, "My country will fall to enemy forces. Perhaps this is the true curse. She is not destroying me. She is destroying Emberfall" (p. 154). Rhen's monstrous form represents a distorted version of his identity that reflects the loss of his agency. This loss of self-control, rather than a physical impairment, is the core of his suffering. Moreover, the magic in the world of *A Curse So Dark and Lonely* is described as "small, harmless", and lacks the extraordinary or transformative abilities commonly associated with magical cures or the creation of disability in traditional fantasy (p. 116). The sorceress' curse is an exception to this characterisation but it is not her magic that provides the cure. Kemmerer's portrayal of Rhen's condition, while not a disability, challenges the stereotypes of disability being either caused by magic or magically cured.

While *A Curse So Dark and Lonely* offers a compelling reinterpretation of the Beauty and the Beast narrative, it is important to acknowledge the inherent limitations of this framework when addressing the complexities of disability representation. While Rhen's curse subverts some conventional tropes, it does not fully escape the stereotypes that often accompany disability in fantasy literature. The curse itself, rooted in magic, is ultimately a problem to be solved through traditional means—a magical cure, catalysed by love. This mirrors many of the tropes that have historically been applied to disabled characters in fantasy: disability as something to be cured or fixed, rather than a condition to be authentically explored and lived with.

In contrast, Harper's experience as a disabled protagonist offers a more nuanced approach to disability in fantasy. While she, too, is part of a larger narrative shaped by her interactions with Prince Rhen and the traditional Beauty and the Beast framework, her journey remains uniquely her own. Harper's disability does not define her character arc nor does it necessitate magical resolution. Rather, her cerebral palsy is a facet of who she is—one that she faces with resilience and resourcefulness, not something to be 'cured' or eliminated by the story's end.

This distinction between Rhen's curse and Harper's disability highlights a broader issue in fantasy literature: the tendency to use magic and love as tools to fix or transform the disabled body. While Kemmerer succeeds in representing a protagonist with cerebral palsy who is strong, capable, and autonomous, the overarching structure of the Beauty and the Beast story still leaves some aspects of disability representation underexplored. *A Curse So Dark and Lonely* marks progress in the representation of disabled characters, and also serves as a reminder that disability metanarratives in fantasy literature require further critical engagement. Moving beyond magic and narrative-driven cures towards more authentic, nuanced portrayals of disability remains a key challenge for the genre.

Conclusion

In *A Curse So Dark and Lonely*, Brigid Kemmerer offers a nuanced exploration of disability, agency, and redemption through the characters of Harper and Rhen. Through Harper, Kemmerer challenges disability stereotypes, portraying her as resilient and autonomous despite her cerebral palsy. Harper's determination and resourcefulness expand what it means to be a protagonist in YA fantasy, demonstrating that disability neither defines nor diminishes her character. Similarly, Rhen's journey of self-discovery and redemption confronts preconceived notions about power and identity in the face of adversity. Despite the limitations of his curse, Rhen learns to embrace vulnerability as a source of strength, offering a poignant contrast to Harper's resilience. Through their intersecting narratives, Kemmerer invites readers to reconsider their perceptions of disability in fantasy literature, urging them to embrace complexity and authenticity in the portrayal of marginalised characters. As the genre continues to evolve, works like *A Curse So Dark and Lonely* serve as important milestones in the ongoing quest for diverse and inclusive representation in YA fantasy.

References

Cheyne, R. (2019) "Fantasy: Affirmation and Enchantment." *Disability, Literature, Genre: Representation and Affect in Contemporary Fiction.* Liverpool University Press.

Kemmerer, B. (2019) *A Curse So Dark and Lonely.* Bloomsbury.

Rutherford, L., Johanson, K. and Reddan, B. (2022) '#Ownvoices, Disruptive Platforms, and Reader Reception in Young Adult Publishing', *Publishing Research Quarterly*, 38(3), pp. 573–585. Available at: https://doi.org/10.1007/s12109-022-09901-5.

Webb, J. (2009) *Understanding Representation.* London: SAGE Publications.

EMILIE MORSCHECK, a Ph.D. candidate at the University of Canberra, investigates the portrayal of autism in young adult fantasy literature. Shortlisted for the 2021 Text Prize and honoured as the inaugural recipient of the Steph Bowe Mentorship for her manuscript 'These Cursed Waters,' her academic pursuits intertwine her passion for writing and research. Emilie's scholarly focus delves into the nuanced representation of autism, aiming to illuminate the intersections of identity and storytelling within the realm of young adult fantasy. Her academic journey embodies a commitment to exploring diverse narratives and advancing understanding of marginalised identities in literature.

---

1. Rutherford, Johanson and Reddan, 2022, p. 575. Since 2015, there has been a significant shift in the language used to discuss disability. For example, the term 'differently-abled' has become less popular, with a preference for 'disabled' as it is seen as more empowering by many in the disability community. Additionally, there has been a greater emphasis on the social model of disability, which focuses on societal barriers rather than individual impairments.
2. Cheyne, p. 114. It is also important to note that terminology around disability varies, and some individuals may prefer different terms to describe their experiences.
3. [1] It is important to note that these narratives are often constructed from the perspective of non-disabled individuals, which can lead to a lack of authentic representation. Negative disability stereotypes in fiction often include the "Bitter Cripple," the "Blind Hag," the "Inspiration Porn" trope, the "Disabled Villain," and the "Magical Disabled Person." The "Bitter Cripple" stereotype appears in modern fiction through characters like Gollum in *The Lord of the Rings*, whose physical disfigurement and bitterness result from his obsession with the One Ring, and Professor X in *X-Men*, who at times reflects a darker version of this archetype, where his paralysis leads to internal conflict and frustration. Moira in *The Handmaid's Tale* also embodies a form of the "Blind Hag," where her emotional and physical scars from oppression represent a metaphorical blindness to hope and the loss of agency in a repressive society (Cheyne, p. 118).
4. Cheyne, p. 113.
5. Webb, p. 7.
6. Cheyne, p. 114.

9

IN THE GRIM DARKNESS OF THE FAR FUTURE...

THERE ARE ONLY WARRIORS

KYLE TAM

 In the grim darkness of the far future, there is only war.

So says the opening blurb that accompanies every piece of media related to Warhammer 40,000, encapsulating the core of what makes this media giant distinct. Across tabletop games, video games, and tie-in novelizations the universe seeks to portray a universal truth of the setting—there is little relief to be found in this far off age. Only conflict. However, whether the darkness is *entirely* grim can vary from author to author, creating a tonal conflict that may make readers uncertain whether the universe should be taken with grave seriousness or be perceived as tongue in cheek. This essay is doing a deep dive into two of the setting's most notable heroes and the disparity between their depictions in the context of this grim future - Ibram Gaunt from the Gaunt's Ghosts series by Dan Abnett and Ciaphas Cain from the Ciaphas Cain novels by Sandy Mitchell. I'll look at how these contrasting approaches have created a fuller universe, as well as how they have vaulted the faction of the Imperium of Man directly into the spotlight of the series as a whole.

THE CORE PREMISE of Warhammer 40,000 is that the universe of the 41st Millennium is in a constant state of warfare enacted by various factions. We have the Eldar, essentially elves as space aliens, the brutish Orks, the eternally ravenous Tyranids, the cybernetic liches known as the Necrons, the harmonious Tau, and of course humankind as represented by the Imperium of Man.[1] Each of these peoples harbors strong hostility for all other groups, believing the rest of space is full of nothing but their enemies. While the tabletop game encapsulates all of these various groups, it is no exaggeration to say that the Imperium of Man is front and center in the universe's stories. With the most figurines, the most material, and the most sympathetic point of view, both within the context of the universe and in our own reality as a fictional group they are considered one of the strongest factions. They are championed most prominently by the Space Marines—genetically engineered supersoldiers who stand head and shoulders above the common man, designed for the sole purpose of protecting the common folk of the Imperium of Man.

Much more than just a tabletop game, Warhammer 40,000 also comprises an entire fictional universe, the Black Library. Within that, two of the most iconic series of the canon are Gaunt's Ghosts and the adventures of Ciaphais Cain. Coincidentally, both series revolve around a commissar who takes charge of a ragtag group of misfits in order to bring acclaim and honor to the Imperium. Their resulting successes vary, as do the trajectories of their lives and, inevitably, their deaths or lack thereof. These series are considered two of the most prominent in the entire bibliography of the Black Library, not only due to the number of volumes in each series but also due to the quality and strength of their writing.

IBRAM GAUNT's claim to fame is in the distinction of taking a number of soldiers who barely amounted to a single regiment and crafting them into the finest of soldiers for the Imperium. In movie terms, it is akin to the drill sergeant who must work magic by taking the chaff and spinning it into gold. Gaunt brings his Ghosts from the Death World of Tanith to the chaos-infested hive world of Vergath, serving at the behest of the human Emperor as all good and noble commissars should do. His work, and the work of his Ghosts, serves as a small peek into what will come to be called the Sabbat World Crusades—the journey to claim foreign planets for the sake of the Imperium's venerated leader.

The book series spans the full period of Gaunt's career, guiding us from the commissar's desperate struggle with a position conferred onto him by his dying predecessor, into the struggle to not only train a disparate group of soldiers but have them be worthy to live and die for their cause. The man himself is only one of a group that includes characters such as the former ganger Tona Criid, the tragically maligned Sniper Rhen Merrt, and the underage regimental musician Brin Milo. This is a series where the Imperial

Guardsmen, otherwise cannon fodder and numbers on a dataslate in the vast conflicts between Inquisitors and Xenos, Space Marines and Chaos, are given faces. Names. Identities. Soldiers who will, as the conflicts rage on, be felled one by one.

By humanizing the Imperial Guardsmen as we explore both their lives and their deaths, we gain greater sympathy with them than with the more alien xenos. The Imperial Guardsmen are also notably forced to face off time and time again with what the world of Warhammer 40,000 deems the forces of Chaos: those soldiers and Space Marines, formerly the rank and file of the Imperium, now tainted by the allure of beings beyond the void. In these clashes with inhumanity Dan Abnett, the author of the Gaunt Series, is able to better emphasize the humanity of his heroes. Flawed, desperate heroes who have been whipped into a fighting force by a single man, to the point that when their commander's suicide mission of atonement is announced they are almost fighting amongst themselves for the chance to die honorably—not for their Emperor, and not for any greater cause, but for a man they know has put himself in danger for them time and time again. In this respect, Gaunt has become something akin to a living saint—a manifestation of a divine will that has been proven to exist but only for the special. The chosen.

Ciaphas Cain, on the other hand, is proclaimed by both his peers and the fans of the Warhammer franchise as not only a hero but THE Hero of the Imperium—greater even than the Emperor himself, though this moniker is somewhat tongue in cheek. He is a man who has escaped certain death at least once per book, both due to his own resourcefulness and a relentless string of good fortune. The man is both self-deprecating and sarcastic, at least on the inside; to the universe at large he is one of the most competent commanders in the universe. But he does not regard himself as a hero: he is quick to rationalize many actions as entirely self-serving, without taking into consideration that heroes are not the type who will proclaim themselves *as* heroes.

From the very first pages of the Ciaphas Cain series, one gets the distinct impression that Ciaphas Cain would truly rather be anywhere else than on the battlefield. He is a man who would be happiest pushing paperwork around or sending out orders, who is instead tasked with that greatest and most horrible of duties—fieldwork. What he has in common with Ibram Gaunt is that though he serves the Imperium, he does not buy fully into its glorious mission. He does not blindly follow orders for the sake of following orders though unlike Gaunt—whose actions are eternally driven by his own sense of duty, heroism, and a desire to do right by the Imperium and those who serve beneath him—his actions are almost entirely for the sake of self-preservation.

LINGUISTICALLY, what makes these two novels quite distinct from each other is that the Gaunt series is told through a shifting third person point of view emphasizing the individual voices of each member of the troop. It creates camaraderie among the chorus; it is military fiction which emphasizes the weight of every body, every voice, felled in combat. The weight of every life lived and, eventually, taken. Meanwhile, Ciaphas Cain's own books are first-person memoirs in which he is free to tell the truth in his thoughts, though annotated, stylized, and commented on both by a trusted aide and then later by historians of the Imperium in order to dissect the thoughts of this most heroic, mysterious, and deeply memed man.

Both of these styles contrast greatly with the almost mythological framing of the Imperium and the religion surrounding its esteemed God-Emperor, the Emperor of Man. Devotion to the Emperor of Man is a religion in and of itself, with warriors rushing into battle boldly declaring that "The Emperor Protects". But the more we see of the worlds through the eyes of our commissars, the less true this maxim holds. The Emperor of Mankind is as distant a deity to his soldiers as any divine being in the records of our own humanity, with the distinction that his Living Saint Celestine, a manifestation of holy faith in the emperor, does exist and takes to the battlefields of her choosing. Those deemed important enough to manifest upon as an act of divine intervention get rescued, while everyone else is forced to get by with nothing but prayer seals, pistols, and hope that the Emperor is with them.

Gaunt and Cain both have literary antecedents. As a franchise that was created in Britain, it is unsurprising that its military leaders are based on prominent figures from British literary tradition. After all, pop cultural references run rampant throughout the narrative tradition of Warhammer 40,000, whether it be from the Dune-esque God Emperor of Man or the Xenomorph-esque designs of the Tyrannids. But it is this easy association with familiar, beloved faces in military fiction that assists in endearing the members of the Imperial Army to the reader.

Gaunt is based on Bernard Cornwell's Richard Sharpe, a sergeant of humble beginnings pulled up by his bootstraps to increasingly harrowing battlefields, with Cornwell's narrative style and writing style felt throughout the series. Like Gaunt, Sharpe is a rank and file soldier elevated to officerhood. But the difference between Sharpe and Gaunt is that the Napoleonic wars were never so filled with desperation and death as the year 40,000, and no soldier was able to return to the battlefield so often as Gaunt's Ghosts are. Being set in the far future allows for the books to half-resurrect their soldiers, prolonging the suffering of their soldiers through the use of advanced medical techniques and mechanical augmentation. One might almost suspect it would have been kinder to allow them to simply die, instead of being returned to the battlefield. But as is common here and throughout the Imperium, one's life does not belong to oneself but to the Emperor.

Ciaphas Cain, on the other hand, is based on George MacDonald Fraser's Harry Flashman, with a touch of Rowan Atkinson's Black Adder. As a character Flashman was known for being a rake, cad and general coward who, through good fortune and coincidence, rises up the ranks to become a decorated general. His, and by extension Cain's, series are characterized by good fortune such as fortuitous circumstances with persons holding the correct equipment or finding a hidden passageway from which one emerges unscathed. What distinguishes between them the most is that Flashman is also a known, or at least exaggerated, womanizer. Cain, on the other hand, may be many things but a reckless lover of woman he is not. There seems less time for flagrant seduction in the grim darkness of the far future, but it also serves to make Cain more heroic than he considers himself.

While the first thing that stands out about Ciaphas Cain is his absolute cowardice in the face of ultimate danger, the second thing that stands out about Cain is that he is no *mere* coward. He has a savviness about his role in the grand schemes of the Imperium, an awareness that if he did not play to the personalities of those around him, he would likely be looking at the wrong end of a gun. In Cain's view, the role of a commissar is as one who is not respected but inevitably stabbed in the back, a person who commands only begrudging respect as fits their station but not any admiration or care for safety. The great irony here is that, though his throughline is focused on his own self-preservation first and foremost, what he inevitably learns is that in order to protect himself he must also protect others.

The underlying thread that runs through the adventures of Ciaphas Cain and Ibram Gaunt is that no matter how ridiculous the situation, how insurmountable the odds they are forced to face, they are able to overcome simply because they are singular existences. Heroes. This immunity does not extend to the rank and file, to the soldiers around them who live and die for want of a nail. No army can exist without soldiers, the Imperium of Mankind included, but there can be no soldiers if they do not believe in the cause.

For "mere" humanity to be able to overcome the vast and desperate odds that have been placed in their way, in a universe riddled with Gods of Chaos and xenos races with superior technological capability, then surely they must have a far greater purpose than these other species?

To an Empire like that of the Imperium, the existence of single leaders and figures of admiration like Cain and Gaunt both are essential. Gaunt's determination in the face of impossible odds and ability to stir the fighting spirit of even the most jaded of soldiers; Cain's survival ability, as well as his supposed leadership skills—these lend credibility to the idea of the resilience of its forces. The Imperium is superior because its people are superior, a creed that in our own reality we have seen reflected in empires beginning from the ancient Babylonian and Greek to the more recent Austro-Hungarian or Imperial Japanese. And in the same vein, great Empires have also elevated the ranks of their most illustrious military officers in order to make this same statement.

> We are superior to you. We will not bow to your will.

There is a certain irony in the contrast between the situations of Cain and Gaunt that makes the two series fascinating to read side by side. Both decorated men who have, by hook or by crook, gone on to achievements of great acclaim. But these are victories not won without sacrifice, and they are not won by one man alone. They are won through the efforts of those around them. One wishes to protect others, but in doing so must sacrifice. The other wishes to protect himself, but in doing so inadvertently protects others. Flawed, yes, but not so flawed that the reader cannot find themselves drawn into the spell cast by the narrative.[2]

But what magic is this that means we, living outside of their universe, see the failures and great flaws of these men as emblematic of their true heroism? In their respective texts, both Gaunt and Cain are considered atypical officers because they are intelligent, resourceful, determined, and charismatic. So what does this say about the "typical" military officer of the Imperium, that those who are able to distinguish themselves are those who eschew the expectations of the post? Possibly the same thing that might be said of military officials in our own reality. Those who keep their head down, follow the letter of the law, and parrot the teachings of those who have come before them without fail will amount to little. These novels offer commentary and satire in equal measure on that which already is, both in the Imperium and in our own reality.

WHAT GAUNT and Cain demonstrate are two very real, and quite cynical, realities in the far future of the 41st Millennium. Both of these men are representatives of the Imperium of Man, of the elevated officers that lead their men to do difficult or even impossible tasks. More than that, they serve as beacons of the shining potential of mankind. Of the cause that they champion. Their heroism is celebrated in the pages, both in-world by friends, foes, and the watching eyes of the Imperium, and out of world by dedicated readers spreading the evangelical word of the Imperium. And even as they do so, they unwittingly peddle the propaganda of fictional forces— seeing heroes where there are merely men, flawed men, doing the dirty work others will not do. Placing them upon an impossible pedestal.

. . .

KYLE IS A WRITER, game designer, and full-time complainer from the Philippines. Her nonfiction has appeared in publications like Interstellar Flight Press, Strange Horizons, *and* Into the Spine. *Her games include the IGDN Honorable Mention* MORIAH, Primadonna *from PlusOneEXP, and* Forsaken *from Afterthought Committee. You can find her on X and Blusky at @PercyPropa, or find her work at* whatkylewrites.carrd.co.

---

1. These disparate races do receive their own viewpoint novels, such as *Da Big Dakka* for the Orks or *The Infinite and the Divine* for the Necrons, but these are clearly written with, for lack of a better word, an alien morality. It becomes harder for the reader to associate with them because the closest cultural parallels they have are hooligans or rogue AI.
2. Then there is the question of where they measure up against the Imperium's finest soldiers— the Adeptus Astartes. The Space Marines, crafted from the gene-seed, the DNA of the Emperor himself and passed down from generation to generation of supersoldiers. To these behemoths of men, on paper even the most worthy of guardsmen should be lesser than they, being made from common stock. However, the balance of power and capability in these books seems far more heavily weighted towards the humble guardsmen, the deaths of Space Marines being utilized merely to show how capable an enemy is. How much greater It is part of the uneven nature of Warhammer 40,000—the flexibility of strength and weakness. The relativity of power in order to showcase the perceived superiority of any given hero, at great odds with the strictly balanced and numerically calculated universe of its parent game.

10

MEN WHO RESPECT WITCHES IV
KINGS, MANHOOD AND MORRIS DANCING

TANSY RAYNER ROBERTS

The theme of respect for witches is embedded deeply in the narrative of *Lords and Ladies*, which is rather ironic given that the subtitle for the novel could easily be "no one gives Magrat enough credit."

Lancre men know that witches deserve respect; certainly there are fewer incidents of mob violence and rebellion against the power of witches in *Lords and Ladies* than we saw in *Wyrd Sisters*.[1]

Jason and Shawn Ogg, representing Ogg adult masculinity,[2] spend their lives in a loose orbit around the authority of witches. These Oggs represent two categories of Lancre men who are strongly featured in this book: Men of the Village (also the Rude Mechanicals/Morris dancers) and Men of the Castle (the King and his servants).

Other significant male roles in the book are filled by Guests From Out of Town and Would-be Suitors (Ridcully the Wizard and Casanunda the dwarf).

Finally there is the Long Man, AKA King of the Elves, AKA the Horned One, apparently the closest thing witches have to a god, and Nanny Ogg's best weapon against the Elf Queen's tyranny.

Let's hope he's feeling respectful to witches, shall we?

(Morris) Men of the Village

Jason, the default patriarch of the Oggs (if they had one, which they do not), is the eldest son of Nanny Ogg.

He holds high status of his own as the village blacksmith — a position layered with trade secrets and mystical knowledge. Jason is the one blacksmith in all the Disc who is trusted to shoe Death's horse — a special and secret honour that he treats with great reverence. Nevertheless, his understanding of the magical world is less nuanced than that of his mother; Nanny struggles to articulate to Jason just how bad elves are, and like many youngsters who were not alive last time the elves came sniffing around, Jason does not fully grasp her message.

Crucially, though, he knows better than to dismiss Nanny's knowledge, even when what she says seems unbelievable.

As a village leader, it falls to Jason to guide his fellow Rude Mechanicals (local craftsmen who are also members of the Lancre Morris Men) when they are called upon to stage a play for the upcoming royal wedding. Despite being the same group of men who regularly tie bells to themselves to perform ceremonial dances, these men are so embarrassed by the play that they take themselves off into the forest to practice secretly.

While this hapless comedy of errors does lead directly to the elf invasion, it is not through the Morris Men's lack of trying to respect the rules laid down by the witches.

Indeed, a healthy fear of Nanny and Granny fuels many of the rehearsal scenes, and the motivations for the group's actions. It is a sign of how powerful the Elf Queen's lure is that the Morris Men are able to overcome their (reasonable) fear of Jason's mam and Granny Weatherwax in order to approach the forbidden standing stones known as the Dancers — where one *must not dance* — all the while convincing themselves that they are staying within the rules *because they do not plan to dance*.

After accidentally unleashing the elves upon Lancre, most of the men are terrified of the Elf Queen and her hordes; Carter the baker, meanwhile, is far more worried about the wrath of Granny Weatherwax.

 "Iron don't have no effect on her! She'll tan our hides for us!"

While mortal song and dance are traditionally used to empower elves, it is dance that the Morris Men are able to weaponise in the final confrontation. The Stick and Bucket Dance, a form of morris which has long been banned in Lancre,[3] becomes the method for the Rude Mechanicals to escape with their lives (and even to fight their way to safety).

A great deal of this book's narrative is devoted to female power, but here the Morris Men are able to use their own power of male community and shared creative arts as an effective if terrifying form of self-defence.[4] Later, at the royal wedding, they all get drunk and do the Stick and Bucket dance again, for themselves, no blood spatter required.

Men of the Castle

The respect offered to the older witches of Lancre by the general community is rarely extended to "young" Magrat, even (especially) after queenship is thrust upon her. Magrat is rightfully frustrated at still being treated like a frivolous airhead who can't be trusted with vital information (eg. the impending danger of elves) or even with decisions about her own future.

King Verence assures his bride-to-be Magrat of his respect for witches,[5] and yet immediately pushes her into pre-made wedding plans without the luxury of a marriage proposal. We later learn, at the same time as Magrat, that Verence was directed to this alarmingly manipulative course by Granny Weatherwax.

It's not a good look. It doesn't help that Verence remains largely unavailable to Magrat during her transition to castle life. They eat "together" but rarely share more than a snippet or two of conversation thanks to the over-large dining table. Verence is busily trying to improve the kingdom and reinvent himself as the Disc's first constitutional monarch, which involves a great deal of book research and consultation with his people (many of whom would prefer not to be consulted, thanks). This shows that Verence is going to turn out a decent king, but gives us little hope he will be a good husband.

Verence has assembled a vague working theory on the role of queens, which he leaves for Magrat and her new maid, Millie, to manage while he gets on with his own work. Millie starts out parroting her mother's idea of "respect" for a queen, but ends up more of an ally in the quest to embrace queenly pursuits. Unfortunately, Verence's (and, to be fair, Magrat's) very shallow understanding of women's history means that their model for the job description of queen leans hard into the kind of patriarchal bullshit that witches usually swerve around.

Apart from a few comic asides about Magrat's attempts to get the (female) castle cook to provide vegetarian options, the rest of the castle staff with any real presence in the story are male.

Shawn Ogg, Nanny's youngest son[6] and Verence's most over-worked servant, quickly falls into a sidekick role for Magrat. Like nearly everyone else, he struggles to see Magrat as any kind of authority. His default is to call her miss, Miss Magrat, or when she pushes him for a more respectful term of address, Miss Queen.

It is Shawn who finally reveals to Magrat the truth about the elves and what a threat they pose to the kingdom. The mortifying experience of having him explain this secret "witch business" to her is the final straw that sends her over the edge into her warrior queen era.

When Shawn is captured and tortured by the elves, Magrat rescues him with extreme violence. After which, he never again has to be reminded to use respectful terms of address.

While Shawn serves the castle with diligence and loyalty, his fealty to his mam Nanny Ogg will always come first. Even when he attempts to maintain guard duty in the face of Nanny's scorn, a single sharp line from Granny Weatherwax has him scrambling to obey.

Another castle servant of note is Hodgesaargh, a gamekeeper whom Magrat consults in the hopes that falconry will be more of a success for her than tapestry.[7] Hodgesaargh is too busy with his own work to show much deference to the new queen, and falconry itself proves to be a letdown for Magrat, confirming her feelings of insignificance.[8] She envies him because he has a clear cut, useful job at the castle, while she does not.

Mr Brooks the beekeeper shows even less respect for (human) royalty — he calls Magrat 'girl' and shows no interest in her status. He is already in thrall to a queen, ruler of the bee swarm, and will not bow to another. It is Mr Brooks who provides Magrat with a model for 'queening' that proves far more useful and inspiring than anything from Verence's books. We are told that Mr Brooks is "as close to a witch as it was possible to be while still being male"[9] due to his access to nature and mystic knowledge. It's probably for the best that he is never placed in opposition to Granny Weatherwax.

These men of the castle may fail repeatedly to show proper respect to Magrat as witch or queen, but it is worth noting that they already exist in worlds where matriarchy is the rule of law — Shawn has deferred to the elder witches his whole life, as has Verence. Mr Brooks appreciates that queens outrank drones. Even Hodgesaargh is at the mercy of his birds of prey. When Hodgesaargh is attacked by the elves, it is his most highly trained raptor, Lady Jane, who saves his life.

Likewise, Nanny Ogg comes to Shawn's rescue when he calls the men of the castle to battle. His grand speech has little effect until after it is peppered by a few discreet after-threats from his mam, ensuring not only a good turnout for the fight, but the preservation of Shawn's pride.

> "Well,' she said. "It's like this. If you go out there you may have to face elves. But if you stops here, you definitely have to face me. Now, elves is worse than me, I'll admit. But I'm persistent.'

Respecting witches, then, is not really an issue for the men of the castle; it is only that Magrat is still not quite seen as worthy of that honour in comparison to her elder peers; at least, not until she is spotted in full armour, terrorising elves with her sword.

Chaps from Out of Town

Both Nanny and Granny receive courting overtures (or at least, gestures in that general direction) from gentlemen visiting Lancre for the wedding.

Once again, Casanunda is a complete delight. This type of male character — the sex-obsessed flirt — rarely ages well in media, and yet Casanunda's pickup lines remain on the comfortable side of enthusiastic consent. His sheer appreciation for Nanny, a woman who is both of a certain age and of a certain weight (not that she is bothered about either of these facts) is highly enjoyable to witness. The awestruck Casanunda adores to watch Nanny eat, drink, and enjoy her life.

> *Nanny Ogg appreciated fine wine in her very own way. It would never have occurred to Casanunda that anyone would top up white wine with port merely because she'd reached the end of the bottle.*

Theirs is a generous romance, written kindly despite the fact that it is a comic relief subplot, with jokes based on the age and size differences of the two maybe-lovers. They enjoy each other's company, and the humour is gentle; this should not feel revolutionary – and yet.

How does Nanny Ogg manage to be the sexiest person in a story full of gorgeous elves? Must be the red boots.

Much as he did in *Witches Abroad*, Casanunda falls easily into a sidekick role, trotting along behind Nanny while she saves the day; even if that means confronting an ancient god under a hill proclaiming the size of his tonker. If Nanny had a handbag, Casanunda would hold it for her.

Ridcully is rather less appealing as a suitor, not least because Granny does not welcome his attempts to woo her. His most romantic gesture, whisking Granny away by teleportation into a private spot in the woods, only to realise he has used up all his magic and can't get them back, is more of a damp squib than a smooth move.[10]

Still, Ridcully is a useful fish out of water character, allowing us a glimpse of Lancre through the eyes of an

Ankh-Morpork resident, albeit one who has been dreamily romanticising his youthful visit to Lancre for at least fifty years.

Their past romance is expressed through a literal chase scene, which has slightly uncomfortable overtones even though the agency of the pursued maiden is made clear (running so fast that he fails to catch her is a miscalculation on her part), and leads young Esme to a far more interesting encounter with the Elf Queen.

Fifty years later,[11] Ridcully is still thinking wistfully about the girl that got away, and Granny Weatherwax is still more interested in what the Elf Queen is up to.

The respect Ridcully offers Granny in the present day is belated and somewhat begrudging; believing he is in the middle of a mature-aged rom com, it takes him some time to realise he is actually a sidekick in a war movie. It takes him even longer to come to terms with the fact that being Archchancellor of Unseen University means next to nothing in this wild little mountain kingdom.

Unlike Casanunda, Ridcully is far too argumentative and resistant to fully accept his sidekick/suitor role, which is why he doesn't get rewarded with a saucy champagne date night. Nevertheless, Ridcully serves the story in reminding us all that the timeline where he did not marry Granny (i.e. this one) is the best of all timelines. If nothing else, she lives longer.

The Husband Under the Hill

The presence of the King of the Elves, AKA the Long Man, is expressed largely as a series of dirty jokes, some of which are literally prehistoric. It is appropriate that we follow Nanny Ogg into the phallic territory of the Elf Queen's other half while accompanied by Casanunda, another repository of dirty jokes.

We are told at the beginning of *Lords and Ladies* that the Elf Queen intends to take a mortal husband to secure her invasion; when warned that the King will not like it, she brushes off any concerns: *"And when has that ever mattered?"*

Indeed, the King shows little interest in his wife's invasion, or the damage she inflicts, until it is drawn to his attention by Nanny Ogg. It is a strange thing, in a novel built around the symbolic might of female power, to conclude with a plot twist where the antagonist's husband is sent to "put a stop" to the threat she poses to the world.

However, there is little about the final act of this novel that disempowers women; as seen in Witches Abroad, Nanny Ogg has never been one to hold back from asking men to share the load when there's work to be done. In this case, Nanny marches into the spiral caves beneath the Long Man (a space specifically devoted to masculine energy)[12] smuggling in iron in the one shape that travels everywhere (a horseshoe, nails and all), demanding that her god step in to stop his wife before the Old Trouble returns.

Nanny offers the King of the Elves nothing in exchange for his help except a reminder that he will never be able to rule the mortal world again; it is progress, not witches, that have doomed him. Still, there is one threatening statement she can make:

> "But I've got kiddies, y'see, and they don't hide under the stairs because they're frit of the thunder, and they don't put milk out for the elves, and they don't hurry home because of the night, and before we go back to the dark old ways, **I'll see you nailed**."

While the Long Man grudgingly respects Nanny's threat (or at least, allows her to get away with it), he also takes his own sweet time about his decision. Thus, the Elf Queen has already been thoroughly beaten by warrior!queen Magrat and the bees and Granny Weatherwax by the time her husband finally bothers to sweep the Queen and her followers back to where they came from.

The task of the Horned One is not to conquer or to subdue his romantic partner, but to quietly clean up her mess and give her a safe place to land once the witches are finished with her.

(And back to the Husband With Bells On)

King Verence, like the Elf King, spends most of the book as a symbol rather than a character. Important moments like Verence's abduction by the Elf Queen happen off the page. Big relationship turning points, like Magrat discovering that he sleeps in front of the door to his kingdom, occur in his absence.

Most of his actual scenes are, however, witch-adjacent.[13] When a wounded Diamanda and the captured elf are brought to the castle, it is Verence and not Magrat who receives a very long and unusually patient explanation on the danger of elves from Granny Weatherwax.

After Verence becomes the Tam Lin to Magrat's Janet, he has no agency or function in his own rescue – unless you count how his compliance with Granny's scheming has so infuriated his future wife that she is able to perform extreme violence against elves.

We never witness a discussion between Magrat and Verence about how he has hurt her; most of her frustration at him in the first half of the book transforms into fury at Granny in the second half. She appears to be prepared to bury the hatchet (battle-axe) once she is allowed to marry him on her own terms, having figured out for herself what kind of queen she is going to be.

Given the high-handed way in which Verence approached their marriage, it is a nice touch that he is convinced (by Granny, of course) to "humble" himself by wearing his Fool's costume for the wedding.[14]

While Verence may have (we can only hope) learned a lesson about the respect due to Magrat, he continues to defer to witches in general, and Granny Weatherwax in particular, in all most important decisions of his reign over Lancre.

 It seemed, in fact, that just as he was about to lower the crown on the bride's head he glanced across the hall to where the skinny old witch was standing. And nearly everyone else did too, including the bride.

The old witch nodded very slightly.

Magrat was crowned.

Tansy Rayner Roberts is a Doctor of Classics, a Doctor Who podcaster, and an author of many science fiction and fantasy books, as well as the essay collection Pratchett's Women. *You can find her at tansyrr.com.*

---

1. From the men, at least — it is the young women of the village, led by Diamanda and incited at least partly by the Queen of the Elves who cause the witches most grief in this particular book.
2. Other men of the family are mentioned in passing, such the sons-in-law who are treated as beloved sons, while the daughters-in-law are terrorised into service, but we only properly meet Jason, Shawn and Young Pewsey the sticky grandson.
3. The joke of the Stick and Bucket Dance, which the Morris Men are not supposed to talk about, is never fully explained; it belongs to the large sub-genre of Pratchett jokes that make the reader's imagination do most of the work. The dance is illegal with women present, falling under the heading of sexual morrisment.
4. Elf defence.
5. As you might recall from *Wyrd Sisters*, Verence's tolerance for listening to the advice of Granny and Nanny was the main reason they put the thumb on the scale to make him king in the first place.
6. Born a decade or so after the death of his father, a fact best not to think about too closely.
7. Having young ladies of Olden Times or Royal Status express frustration and boredom about the expectation that they should produce masterworks of needlecraft is one of the weirdest of all possible fantasy tropes, which we can't even blame on men. Female writers are just as guilty when it comes to using 'too cool for embroidery' as a shorthand for 'protagonist'. An egregious recent example of this is found in Season 1 of *Bridgerton*, where the professional modiste refers dismissively to embroidery skills as an example of how useless

ladies are! The *audacity*! Try telling that to Jane Austen, and she'd beat you around the head with a bonnet she trimmed herself.

8. As a queen, she is only allowed to use a fainting, wheezing wowhawk... unlike witches, who have no formal falconry status at all.
9. We would not properly meet a male example of a witch (or at least, a witch in training) until Geoffrey Swivel comes to Tiffany's attention in the final Discworld novel *The Shepherd's Crown*; here in *Lords and Ladies*, it is interesting the mystical status of men like Jason and Mr Brooks are alluded to as close to witchcraft without any reference to the quite different magic employed by wizards.
10. See "Celibacy & the Single Wizzard," in this collection.
11. Cough, or is it seventy? Thirty? Let's not talk about time travel, shall we?
12. "Very mackko (sic) place, this," she comments in her worldly manner.
13. Apart from a tiny subplot in which Verence and Magrat are desperate to learn about how to perform on their wedding night without consulting the elder witches, but the book he sends away for is about Martial Arts, not Marital Arts, and thus is of more use to Shawn Ogg who unwraps the parcel by accident. Thank goodness Verence has the opportunity for a quiet chat with Casanunda!
14. Can we interpret this as a kind of sideways apology/wedding gift from Granny Weatherwax? After all, Magrat fell in love with a Fool, and it's largely Granny's fault that she ended up having to marry a King instead.

11

THE DUBLIN PORTAL...
OR THE DUBLIN INTRUSION?

VAL NOLAN

STYLED as the kind of 'sufficiently advanced technology' that's 'indistinguishable from magic' which Science Fiction and Fantasy has rehearsed for decades,[1] the Dublin/New York Portal—an interactive public video installation—represents a sincere artistic effort to flatten the curvature of spacetime by bringing together cities geographically distant and temporally out of synch, while, in the process, encouraging people to 'rethink the meaning of unity'.[2] A freestanding 3.4 meter circular screen livestreaming images across the world, this 'technology art sculpture'[3] is one of several envisioned by Lithuanian artist Benediktas Gylys (with the object itself designed by engineers at the Creativity and Innovation Centre at Vilnius Gediminas Technical University).[4] The Dublin Portal on the city's North Earl Street was established with the collaboration of Dublin City Council in May 2024. Its corresponding screen was initially placed on the Flatiron South Public Plaza at the intersection of Broadway, Fifth Avenue, and 23rd Street in New York City (though it has now been moved to Philadelphia). Yet the Portal's name, though evocative, is misleading. This may seem a petty, even pedantic observation (shout-out to fellow academics!), but it is a worthy consideration insofar as, had it been framed or discussed differently from the outset, many of the issues which arose in Dublin could have been more readily predicted. Because, despite its name, the Portal does not allow us to physically transition from 'familiar surroundings' into 'an unknown place' (*à la* television's Stargate, which it superficially resembles).[5] Indeed, in the case of the Dublin Portal, the on-street participant is firmly enmeshed in their mundane reality and instead of the movements of 'entry, transition, and exploration', the installation relies instead on 'the illusion of presence' generated by a real-time video link.[6] It thus teases us with the possibility of stepping through but in fact *denies* us the satisfaction of the threshold moment; we can walk right up to it, but we can never cross its event horizon. Or at least we could walk up to it until bad behaviour put an end to that, and so we are doubly denied. Triply denied, even, insofar as what the Portal does offer is an alluring mirage, mere echoes of real people manifesting without corporality like so many ghosts of the Gothic tradition.

So, if it is *not* a portal, what is it? Certainly columnist Fintan O'Toole in *The Irish Times* was on to something when he identified the sense of 'magical smoothing of time' and 'frictionless fusion of spaces' as the Portal's key characteristics.[7] Such an appeal to the language and imagery of speculative fiction unlocks a useful critical apparatus for interpreting this project. Indeed, in applying these resources we can see that the Dublin Portal can be identified as, to use the terminology of Farah Mendlesohn in *Rhetorics of Fantasy* (2008), the physical manifestation of an intrusion fantasy.[8] The

Dublin Portal in fact fits Mendlesohn's description quite neatly:

> The trajectory of the intrusion fantasy is straightforward: the world is ruptured by the intrusion, which disrupts normality and has to be negotiated with or defeated, sent back whence it came, or controlled.[9]

It is, of course, unconventional to apply a rhetorical or even poetic analysis to a physical object 'hosted in the primary world' (meaning, in this case, our reality), however there are grounds to do so in how Gylys's circular installation is clearly *informed* by speculative fiction and deliberately appeals to its terminology and imagery.[10] It permits a slice of asynchronous space and time to impinge upon everyday life in a manner which mimics aspects of not just the Stargate, but also Galadriel's mirror in *The Lord of the Rings*, *Star Trek*'s Guardian of Forever—which, not for nothing, also had a connection to New York City—as well as the portals of *Doctor Strange*, and many, many others. Second, to deploy Mendlesohn's rhetorical analysis in discussion of a physical object is to embrace her own assertion that a critical study should 'open up new lines of inquiry' and even 'lay down new challenges'.[11] This is especially true given how the sense of rupture, *dis*ruption, negotiation, and control typical of intrusion fantasies are all present in an account of events in Dublin. Finally, though the Dublin Portal is not a narrative, it is consciously offered as a medium *for* narrative, and, somewhat fulfilling Mendlesohn's observation that intrusion tales tend to be club stories (those being 'tales told within an enabling frame-story to a group of companions in a sheltered venue'), we can note how the Portal was portrayed as having a social and communicative significance.[12] Gylys, through his non-profit foundation, constructed a narrative around the project by which he convinced partner organisations, such as Dublin City Council, of the merits of the portal installations. Indeed, this careful cultivation of the Portal as a vehicle for narrative (even entertainment) helped the project avoid the contested reception of some other public art installations in Ireland (particularly those involving technological apparatus; the river Liffey's ill-fated Millennium Clock, 1996, is the obvious example).[13] As such, the Portal makes manifest a series of stories, on the one hand the story of contemporary visitors interacting with each other across the screens/world and, on the other, the longstanding connection between two distant locations (Ireland and New York, the latter historically a kind of Fantasyland for the Irish working class or even, to borrow another of Mendlesohn's categorisations, an *immersive* fantasy of sorts for them, but that is a topic for another day).

Viewed in this light, it is clear how the Portal ruptures the epistemological mesh in which the day-to-day lives of Dubliners are embedded via an intrusion-style sense of 'two world-layers interacting' (with the ripples of this percolating like interference waves across the country and beyond through media coverage).[14] The appearance of New York on a Dublin street appears to break physical laws of space and time as a precursor to breaking the accepted norms of common decency—the poor behaviour of some people before the Portal—which in turn upset the 'moral universe' on which Gylys's fantasy of connection is predicated.[15] In the process, it makes strange what Mendlesohn calls 'the intimacy of the relationship between people and their surroundings'.[16] We must literally negotiate the material presence of this large object on the street by walking around it but, more than that, we must cognitively negotiate its presence by *thinking* around it. We must account for its disquieting attempt to destabilise the "now" by linking, if only virtually, two different time zones—Dublin by night, New York by day—both of which have an equal claim to the primacy of the present moment. We must parse the unexpected visual dissonance—a yellow taxicab on a Dublin street, for instance—which wrongfoots our brain's ability to define North Earl Street as a single physical location. We must reconcile how the installation's position on a public throughfare grants it a communal quality yet also allows it to casually violate the privacy of the passing individual who may not wish to be seen on a screen by someone five thousand kilometres away, like Samwise Gamgee leaning over Galadriel's mirror, seeking 'a glimpse of what's going on at home'.[17] For, as well meaning as it may be, this intrusion is a carrier wave for eyes, for voyeurs, and for the judgement of others (always a particularly disruptive occurrence in Ireland). It is, in some ways, the ultimate twitching curtain.

More pointedly, of course, an intrusion in speculative fiction is usually 'the bringer of chaos', and this too is true of the Dublin Portal. Indeed, this is where our identification of the installation with Mendlesohn's description becomes most pronounced.[18] Or, to borrow the variously attributed genre adage, this is where we realise that a good science-fiction story should be able to predict not just the automobile but the traffic jam. In this case, the Dublin Portal quickly became 'a magnet not just for passersby but for exhibitionists. Flesh has been bared. Drugs have been performatively consumed. Provocative images have been held up for display. As a result, the portal [was] temporarily closed'.[19] The human element thus problematised O'Toole's 'frictionless fusion of spaces' in headline-grabbing fashion as the transformative power of many a charmed circle to make us all into performers exerted itself in edge cases which nonetheless dominated the discourse.[20] During its first weeks, the Portal took on—in the broadest understanding of these terms—the 'sense of threat, of waiting' which Mendlesohn identifies with intrusion narratives; it enabled bad behaviour which became, with a beautiful sense of irony, symbolic of exactly the stereotypical Irish inability to conduct ourselves which the installation's openhanded gesture towards global interconnectedness sought to reject.[21] The ringlike structure of the Portal simultaneously offered 'a sense of a protected space, one that cannot be ruptured, and a sense that such a rupture is imminent'.[22] It created the impression of a gap in spatial and civil reality, a vacuum into which the people seen through screen seem to withdraw from us into two-dimensional representations. They are a mystery (yes, even if they are a friend or family member whom we have arranged to "meet" through the video link). They are unreal, an uncanny personification of absence, indeed of lifelessness, which many sought to combat in uninhibited fashion. 'Videos circulating online included clips of a man "mooning" and others apparently pretending to take drugs. A caller to [Irish national broadcaster] RTÉ told of a woman suspected of being under the influence of alcohol being led away by Gardaí [the Irish police] after dancing provocatively against the portal screen'.[23] In this way the initial delight surrounding the Portal's presence soon became concern. Concern quickly became fear. And, to paraphrase an observation by the great Roz Kaveney, 'intimacy of seduction' became 'intimacy of disgust'.[24] The latent potential for bad behaviour soon became ever present at the Portal site, such as when *The Irish Times* attended it to find that 'a group of twentysomethings were taking turns to post pornographic images up to the camera lens and laughing to themselves [but] there was no garda in sight'.[25] In intrusion fashion, the sensation that something just offscreen could burst into sight at any time began to define the experience of the Portal. In the worst instances, 'some people on the Irish side have thrown eggs, flashed body parts and displayed images of swastikas and the twin towers burning on 9/11', promoting one New York tabloid to melodramatically declare it a 'portal to hell' (though, to be fair, body parts were infamously flashed from *both* sides of the connection).[26]

Such events—and the resulting press coverage—rapidly prompted both practical and symbolic efforts to negotiate with and control the intrusion. The solution of the authorities was, in fact, hilariously on the nose for how Mendlesohn describes intrusion fantasies as 'structured around punishment and the danger of transgression'.[27] With the nonconsensual and inappropriately public display of body parts a particular issue, what was instigated was an almost Gothic style 'punishment for sexual activity'.[28] This fix—which involved blurring the Portal screen once someone gets too close to the event horizon—ironically inverts the usual relationship between sight and distance; instead of proximity bringing clarity it now brings obfuscation. An Icarian visitor who peers too closely into the aperture now has the image hidden from them, and, again, it is remarkable how precisely Mendlesohn anticipates this appearance of latency: 'the withholding, not of information, but of visuals or events'.[29] Such suppression represents a response to the unsettling concern of the Powers That Be that there is 'always something lurking'.[30] Thus the imposition of a liminal space in front of the Portal—both by blurring algorithms in Dublin and by physical barriers on the New York side—places it further out of reach even as members of the public are steered away from the event horizon by literal gatekeepers 'tasked with minding the portal to deter troublemakers and manage over-enthusiastic onlookers' by utilising a phone app that 'allows them to turn the portal on and off whenever they need'[31] (or, as Galadriel warned, 'Do not touch the water!'[32]). What all of this does, however, is emphasise the manner by which the Portal 'only transmits images' and not sound.[33] Thus there is initially one crucial element of Mendlesohn's intrusion definition which appears missing from the Portal experience. That is aurality, the manner by which an intrusion 'creates response directly through the sound of the world, the sound of horror, of fear, or of surprise'.[34] Two points are, however, worth considering. First, silence is still an aural experience, and an often unsettling one at that. Insubstantial figures moving without sound and seeming to gesticulate in an obscure manner have, after all, long been a reliable ghost story trope. Second, and perhaps more importantly, Mendlesohn's aurality can be readily transcribed onto the cacophony of media responses to the bad behaviour which the Portal engendered.[35] Like characters in a story, many in the media reacted in escalating mock horror to events on the edge of the intrusion: 'Dubliners mortified by antics at capital's transatlantic portal', reported one article.[36] 'Has the city "disgraced ourselves again"' asked another.[37] Or, in the words of one Portal attendant quoted online, 'it's been a lot of ass'.[38]

The resultant pearl-clutching puts one in mind of another infamous reaction to an intrusion narrative in Dublin, the disorder which accompanied the 1907 opening performance of JM Synge's play *The Playboy of the Western World* (the play portrays a small west of Ireland village disrupted by the arrival of a stranger who fast becomes a kind of romanticised folk hero after claiming to have murdered his seemingly tyrannical father; the story quickly proceeds through the familiar pattern of rupture, disruption, negotiation, and control). This classic intrusion narrative resulted, like the Dublin Portal, in real-world public disquiet when a series of riots were instigated by those who deemed the play—which is amazing, you should see it—to be offensive to public morals, particularly in its mention of women's undergarments (the resulting disarray in the theatre caused portions of the play to be acted out in dumb show, an eerie anticipation of the silent movements of the figures on the Dublin Portal screen). Yet while the city's riotous response to art has evolved into op-eds and talk-show discussions over the past hundred years, a curious similarity can nonetheless be observed: an intrusion has permitted us to see not a distant land—be that rural Mayo or glimmering Manhattan—but instead has offered up a vantage on ourselves (and our undergarments... or lack thereof) as Dubliners saw their fellow citizens seize an opportunity to ape the disruptive bravado of the *Playboy*'s protagonist. Thus intrusion theory offers a measure of context for responses to the instances of acting out which occurred, and there we find the true benefit of reframing the Dublin Portal as the Dublin Intrusion. Like *The Playboy of the Western World* did for Ireland more generally, the installation offers a 'mirror on a city's soul'.[39] It does not show New York to Dublin so much as it shows Dublin to itself; what it allows for is critical introspection on the contradictions of contemporary Irish identity, a self-identifying progressive society still struggling with a historically conservative mentality and with more than a share of postcolonial angst. Here the issue of aurality acquires renewed relevance. The decision by Gylys for the Portal installations to transmit visuals from distant locations but not sound ensures that we cannot appeal to the other. It instead forces us—as good art always does—into dialogue with ourselves. Forces us, in fact, to *confront* ourselves.

Thus escalating in intensity in accordance with Mendlesohn's description of the form, the intrusion made its presence felt far beyond North Earl Street as it moved 'into the lives of very ordinary people'.[40] Families found themselves eating breakfast alongside the intrusion as its image saturated newspaper pages and television screens. People driving home from work found themselves carsharing with the intrusion as radio shows debated the antics it had inspired. Dubliners and regular visitors to the capital found themselves straying from their usual routes to see the intrusion with their own eyes. It has even begun to impinge upon contemporary fiction, making an appearance as a 'very *Star Trek*-y' object that 'might have to be shut down on account of the carry on' in a recent story by Mary O'Donnell.[41] Yet, in seeking to exorcise this intrusion's more troublesome aspects from our public and private spaces, in seeking to control it with blurring algorithms and attendants, what exactly are we attempting to do? Are we seeking to preserve public decency (a slippery slope, though it should be noted that while there are consensual and age-appropriate spaces for some of the activities which occurred, such as bared bodies, a city centre street is not one of them)? Are we looking to safeguard transatlantic relations ('it may be inflicting damage upon the general relations and public perceptions between the people of New York, the US, and the people of Dublin', claimed one complainant)?[42] Perhaps we are attempting to maintain an idea of ourselves which has, Synge-style, been challenged more than we are comfortable with ('What are people going to think of us?' bemoans one character in O'Donnell's story)?[43] All of these are, to one extent or another, part of our wider negotiation with the intrusion and with Ireland's place in the globalised world which it makes visible, one that transcends technical adjustments or the hiring of onsite staff. Yet any such self-reflection on our motivation may benefit from also pondering 'the naïveté' upon which Mendlesohn sees intrusion narratives depending.[44] Though in this case, it is difficult to know who has been the *most* naïve. Perhaps it is the 'idealistic' artists and engineers attempting to 'counter polarising ideas and to communicate that the only way for us to continue our journey on this beautiful spaceship called Earth is together'.[45] Perhaps it is Dublin City Council, who seem to have initially underestimated the potential for lewd acts and then scrambled to respond to bad press and bad behaviour. Or, just maybe, it is academics attempting to decouple rhetorical analysis from text in an effort to better understand aspects of the wider world. Next up, perhaps, the Dublin Port Tunnel as Portal Quest?

Val Nolan is a Research Fellow at Aberystwyth University. He is co-author of the SFFH writing-guide series Spec-Fic for Newbies (*Luna Press, 2023, 2024*) *and author of the monograph* Neil Jordan: Works for the Page (*Cork University Press, 2022*). *His academic articles have appeared in* Science Fiction Studies, Irish University Review, Journal of Graphic Novels and Comics, Irish Studies Review, Foundation, Symplokē, *and elsewhere. His own fiction has been published in* Year's Best Science Fiction, Best of British Science Fiction, Interzone, *the 'Futures' page of* Nature, *and* Andromeda Spaceways, *among other venues. He writes the regular 'Folded Spaces' column for* Interzone *exploring the history of Science Fiction criticism.*

---

1. Clarke, Arthur C. *Astounding Days: A Science Fictional Autobiography*. London: Gollancz, 1989. This "law" was first mentioned in the revised edition of Clarke's *Profiles of the Future*, 1982.
2. Lyons, Kim. Vilnius, 'Lithuania built a "portal" to another city to help keep people connected', *The Verge*, 30 May 2021 <https://www.theverge.com/2021/5/30/22460964/vilnius-lithuania-portal-poland-connection-pandemic> accessed 20 January 2025.
3. Portals Organisation. <https://www.portals.org/> Accessed 21 January 2025.
4. Lyons.
5. Farah Mendlesohn, *Rhetorics of Fantasy*, p. 1.
6. Mendlesohn, p. 2, 1.
7. Fintan O'Toole, 'Dublin portal reminds us that our capital has an uneasy edge of wildness', *The Irish Times*, 18 May 2024, <https://www.irishtimes.com/life-style/people/2024/05/18/fintan-otoole-dublin-portal-reminds-us-that-our-capital-has-an-uneasy-edge-of-wildness/> accessed 18 May 2024.
8. Mendlesohn, p. 114.
9. Mendlesohn, p. 115.
10. Mendlesohn, p. 114.
11. Mendlesohn, p. 246.
12. Clute, John. 'Club Story'. *The Encyclopedia of Science Fiction*. Eds. John Clute and David Langford. Ansible Editions, 29 July 2024 <sf-encyclopedia.com/entry/club_story> accessed 5 February 2025.
13. See this article for a summary of what happened with the Millennium Clock: Egan, Rory. 'The Millennium Clock'. Irish Independent, 2 April 2006 <https://www.independent.ie/news/the-millennium-clock/26410316.html> accessed 6 February 2025.
14. Mendlesohn, p. 120.

15. Mendlesohn, p. 5.
16. Mendlesohn, p. 129.
17. Tolkien, JRR. *The Lord of the Rings* (50th Anniversery Edition), p 362.
18. Mendlesohn, p. xxi.
19. Editorial, 'The *Irish Times* view on the Dublin Portal: mirror on a city's soul', *The Irish Times*, 16 May 2024 <https://www.irishtimes.com/opinion/editorials/2024/05/16/the-irish-times-view-on-the-dublin-portal-mirror-on-a-citys-soul/> accessed 17 May 2024.
20. O'Toole.
21. Mendlesohn, p. 130.
22. Mendlesohn, p. 117.
23. Sharkey, Kevin, and McBride, Mike. A "small minority" ruining Dublin Portal experience', *BBC News*, 14 May 2024 <https://www.bbc.com/news/articles/cd1882x5xgg0> accessed 23 January 2025.
24. Mendlesohn, p. 144. Mendlesohn attributes the observation to a phone conversation with Kaveney.
25. McGreevy, Ronan. 'What now for the Dublin Portal? Has the city "disgraced ourselves again" over the art installation?' *The Irish Times*, 18 May 2024 <https://www.irishtimes.com/ireland/dublin/2024/05/18/what-now-for-the-dublin-portal-has-the-city-disgraced-ourselves-again-over-the-art-installation/> accessed 24 January 2025.
26. Carroll, Rory. *The Guardian*. 'Dublin video portal to New York shuts temporarily due to unruly behaviour', 14 May 2024 <https://www.theguardian.com/artanddesign/article/2024/may/14/dublin-video-portal-to-new-york-shuts-temporarily-due-to-unruly-behaviour> accessed 15 December 2024.
27. Mendlesohn, p. 5.
28. Mendlesohn, p. 125.
29. Mendlesohn, p. 116.
30. Mendlesohn, p. 116.
31. Maguire, Mairead. '"It's been a lot of ass": Reflections on 100 days of the Dublin-New York portal', *The Journal*, 9 August 2024 <https://www.thejournal.ie/portal-dublin-new-york-dublin-city-council-6457979-Aug2024/> accessed 24 January 2025.
32. Tolkien, p. 362.
33. Ikeda, Emilie, and Fitzgerald, Meagan. 'Tears, laughs and bare butts beamed through portal linking Dublin and New York'. *NBC News*, 16 May 2024 <https://www.nbcnews.com/news/world/the-portal-rcna152199> accessed 9 January 2025.
34. Mendlesohn, p. 121.
35. Sharkey and McBride.

36. Gallagher, Fiachra. '"Move it to the South Side": Dubliners mortified by antics at capital's transatlantic portal', *The Irish Times*, 25 July 2024 <https://www.irishtimes.com/ireland/2024/07/25/dubliners-mortified-by-antics-at-capitals-transatlantic-portal/> accessed 25 January 2025.
37. McGreevy.
38. Maguire.
39. Editorial, *The Irish Times*, 16 May 2024.
40. Mendlesohn, p. 141.
41. O'Donnell, Mary. 'Edna', in *Walking Ghosts* (Dublin: Mercier, 2025), pp. 139-143 (p. 140).
42. Gallagher.
43. O'Donnell, p. 140.
44. Mendlesohn, p. 115.
45. O'Toole.

12

SHOULD GALADRIEL HAVE TAKEN THE RING?

NICK HUBBLE

THE FOURTH AGE under the dominion of men isn't going too well, is it? Did the free peoples of Middle-earth really combine to overthrow Sauron so that the world would be delivered on a plate to the likes of Donald Trump and Elon Musk? I think not. But how might things have worked out differently? One alternative not discussed at the Council of Elrond is that Galadriel might take the ring. While Elrond does say, 'If any of the Wise should with this Ring overthrow the Lord of Mordor using his own arts, he would set himself on Sauron's throne, and yet another Dark Lord would appear',[1] Galadriel is not a 'he'. Moreover, she is not even from the same type of story as Gandalf, Aragorn and Faramir, male characters who demonstrate their goodness by refusing to take the ring when they have the opportunity. For Galadriel is clearly a figuration of the Fairy Queen in the same way that Lórien, the enchanted realm she rules in which time passes in a different manner to outside its borders, is a figuration of fairy land or Faery, as it is sometimes known.[2]

Tolkien's obsession with Faery can be traced from his first published work, the poem 'Goblin Feet' (1915), to virtually his last, Smith of Wootton Major (1967), in which the titular character dances with an elven maiden in Faery and only towards the end of his life comes to realise that she was the Fairy Queen. He knew the medieval poem Sir Orfeo, described by Maureen Duffy as 'the first unequivocal description of fairyland'.[3] The key features of that description – the Fairy King and the hunt and ride – inform the depiction of the wood elves' kingdom in The Hobbit.[4] Duffy argues that the persistence of such fairy tales in English culture is because they provided an imaginative alternative to the Christianity which became dominant over the course of the Middle Ages. In particular, they expressed the unconscious desire for greater sexual freedom that had been experienced historically in connection to the considerable female agency found in earlier Anglo-Saxon and Celtic pagan cultures.[5] The 'beautiful, idealized and forbidden mother-figure' of the Fairy Queen,[6] who provides for her human lover's food and clothing before abandoning him on the cold hillside to pine away for the unattainable, went on to become a staple of English literature from Spenser to Keats. While not appropriate for The Hobbit, her inclusion in The Lord of the Rings marks the point when it is clear that the story is moving into more adult territory than its precursor.

Although Galadriel does not accept the ring when Frodo offers it to her, her refusal takes a rather different form to that of the male characters in the novel. She is not afraid to admit that she has long desired it and momentarily we see what she might become with it: 'She stood before Frodo seeming now tall beyond measurement, and beautiful beyond enduring, terrible and worshipful'.[7] Immediately afterwards, though, she appears once more a slender elf-woman and reflects that she has passed the test and will therefore diminish and return to the West. But are these appearances and reflections what they seem? Is she really diminished? Only a few pages later, as the fellowship depart from Lórien, Galadriel reveals herself again to Frodo as 'a queen, great and beautiful, but no longer terrible'.[8] Exactly what 'test' she might have passed is one of the most enigmatic riddles in Tolkien's work.

As Christopher Tolkien notes in his editorial introduction to 'The History of Galadriel and Celeborn' in Unfinished Tales: 'There is no part of the history of Middle-earth more full of problems than the story of Galadriel and Celeborn.'[9] However, the root cause of this problem is not just that Galadriel and Celeborn were invented during the course of writing The Lord of the Rings and had no prior existence in the wider body of work that would eventually be published as The Silmarillion, but also that Galadriel, as Faery Queen, sits outside Tolkien's binary moral framework. He therefore had considerable difficulty with inserting her seamlessly into The Lord of the Rings, let alone with retrofitting her into the existing tales of his wider legendarium. Unsurprisingly, he was still attempting to fix Galadriel's story in the last months of his life.[10]

The first reference to Lórien in The Lord of the Rings comes when Elrond's scouts return to Rivendell before the departure of the fellowship. We are told that 'the sons of Elrond, Elladen and Elrohir, were the last to return; they had made a great journey, passing down the Silverlode into a strange country'.[11] However, this makes little sense because Galadriel is the grandmother of Elladen and Elrohir, to whom Lórien would be well known and not at all a 'strange country'. In other words, this sentence is one of the surviving traces – rather like the fox in the Shire who wonders to himself what is going on[12] – of Tolkien's earliest drafts from the late 1930s. If we turn to the first versions of the chapters set in Lórien, we find that Aragorn has no knowledge of Galadriel or even if elves still live in the woods at all.[13] When, after the first meeting of the fellowship with Galadriel, Boromir expresses his doubts of this elvish lady and her purposes, Aragorn does not offer the stern rebuke of the published version but merely replies, 'Well, whatever you may think of the Lady, she was a friend of Gandalf, it seems'.[14]

When Frodo offers her the ring in this first draft, Galadriel's 'sudden clear laugh' is 'of pure merriment,'[15] which recalls the playful attitude of another 'friend of Gandalf', Tom Bombadil. In many ways, her initial role in the novel appears to be equivalent to that of Bombadil – the two have a similar line count even in the published version – with both characters embodying aspects of English folk lore encountered by the hobbits on their quest. This sense of Galadriel as the Fairy Queen is further reinforced when Faramir learns from Frodo and Sam that his brother Boromir had passed through Lórien and met Galadriel, 'the Lady that dies not'. He reflects: 'If men have dealings with the Mistress of Magic who dwells in the Golden Wood, then they may look for strange things to follow. For it is perilous for mortal men to walk out of the world of this Sun, and few of old came thence unchanged, 'tis said'.[16]

The idea of Lórien as Faery is strengthened by the relatively late addition during the writing of The Lord of the Rings of the relationship between mortal Aragorn and elven Arwen (in the early drafts, Aragorn was to marry Éowyn of Rohan[17]). As related in Appendix A,[18] Aragorn is raised as a son by Elrond following the death of his father, but he doesn't meet Elrond's daughter Arwen until he is fully grown because she has been living with her grandmother Galadriel in Lórien. When she returns to Rivendell, Aragorn falls in love with her. However, as Elrond explains to him, a doom is laid on Arwen and her brothers that they shall only stay immortal elves while their father remains in Middle-earth. If Elrond leaves for the West, his children need to choose between accompanying him or remaining in Middle-earth as mortals. On hearing this, Aragorn leaves Rivendell and spends thirty years fighting against the forces of Sauron. At last, coming to the borders of Lórien, he is admitted into that 'hidden land' by Galadriel, who clothes him in silver and white, with a gem on his brow so that he looks like an Elf-lord from the Isles of the West. In this state, he once again meets Arwen, who now falls in love with him. Together, they wander the enchanted glades of Lórien until on Midsummer's Eve, barefoot among the elanor and niphredil on the hill of Cerin Amroth, they plight their troth. When Frodo comes upon him at the foot of Cerin Amroth during the fellowship's stay in Lórien, Aragorn, holding a single golden bloom of elanor, is lost in the 'fair memory' of those days: 'Here is the heart of Elvendom on earth', he says before leaving the hill and coming there 'never again as a living man'.[19] The sense we have that he will never regain access to this enchanted world again is typical of this type of fairy tale, but Tolkien compounds the sense of loss with a tragic twist. For it is the now-mortal Arwen who, following Aragorn's eventual death many years later, finds herself wandering in search of the enchanted memory of Lórien from which she is forever locked out, before laying herself down weeping to die on the cold hillside of Cerin Amroth amidst the fallen mallorn-leaves. It is a hard story. Indeed, Tolkien eventually toned it down by revising the appendices for the second edition of The Lord of the Rings, so that Arwen appears less nakedly distraught. Nevertheless, her fate reinforces the extent to which the 'Return of the King' enacted by the novel represents the overcoming not just of Sauron but also of the world of Faery. Rather than the marriage of Arwen and Aragorn marking an alliance between Faery and the world of mortal men, it serves mainly to subsume the symbolic power of Arwen's matrilinear descent from Galadriel within the patrilinear genealogy of Aragorn's (and his sons' and their sons') lineage, which stretches back unbroken to the earliest rulers of elves and men.[20]

We can trace the matrilinear line of descent from Arwen to Galadriel similarly far back through one of Tolkien's attempts to account for Galadriel's history, in which he described her as 'a handmaid of Melian the immortal in the realm of Doriath' in the First Age.[21] Melian, like Gandalf and Sauron, was one of the semi-divine Maia and originally dwelt in the first Lórien, a beautiful garden of visions and dreams within the heart of Valinor, where she was renowned for her love of birds and skill in songs of enchantment.[22] When elves first awakened in Middle-earth, Melian left Valinor with her birds to fill the silence before dawn with their singing. Here, her singing attracted Elwë Thingol, who would later be the king of the Sindar, the Grey Elves. Losing all other purpose, he followed the sound of her voice until he came upon her in a woodland glade open to the stars, took her hand and 'straightaway a spell was laid upon him' so that he stood still with her while many years passed and the elves he was with passed over the seas to Valinor.[23] Together, Melian and Thingol established and ruled over the kingdom of Doriath, which like Faery was kept hidden and defended by her powers of enchantment. Later, Galadriel lived with them, becoming very close to Melian 'and of her learned great lore and wisdom concerning Middle-earth'.[24] The implication of the phrase in Tolkien's drafts that there 'was much love between them'[25] is that their relationship became akin to that of mother and daughter with Galadriel going on to assume the role of Melian's successor in Middle-earth and to found Lórien as a replacement for Doriath.

Despite the relationship between them in the texts, however, Melian and Galadriel are clearly both incarnations of the Fairy Queen and therefore occupy the same role in Tolkien's symbolic thinking. The very first stories of what would become The Silmarillion, written by Tolkien while convalescing towards the end of the First World War, feature the mortal man Beren entering Doriath (Faery) and falling in love with Lúthien, the daughter of Melian (the Fairy Queen) and Thingol. An angry Thingol tells Beren that he can only marry Lúthien if he can steal one of the Silmarils from Morgoth's crown. After many adventures, Beren and Lúthien do succeed in stealing the Silmaril, although in the aftermath they both lose their lives. However, the Valar intervene and award them a second lifetime to live together, which they do far from the sight of elves and men, but the price is that Lúthien, like Arwen millennia after her, must endure a mortal death and leave the world forever. The structural symmetry between the fairy stories of Beren and Lúthien (and Melian) and Aragorn and Arwen (and Galadriel) strongly implies that it is only possible for an immortal elf woman to live with a mortal man by rejecting Faery and the rule of the Fairy Queen and choosing to live by the rules of men.

Galadriel was not just the Third Age equivalent of Melian, but also one of the leaders of the Noldor, the High Elves, who in the First Age rebelled against the Valar by declaring war on Morgoth for his theft of the Silmarils. It is implied by the song she sings when the fellowship leaves Lórien,[26] and was later explicitly stated by Tolkien in his notes to The Road Goes Ever On, that 'after the overthrow of Morgoth at the end of the First Age a ban was set on her return [to Valinor], and she had replied proudly that she had no wish to do so'.[27] After trying out various combinations, and finally deciding on Galadriel being the sister rather than daughter of Finrod, he allows her to imply that she met Celeborn in the woods that would become Lórien: 'for ere the fall of Nargothrond or Gondolin I passed over the mountains, and together through ages of the world we have fought the long defeat'.[28] In this manner, Tolkien was able to provide a partial explanation for the relative lack of involvement of Galadriel in the events recounted in The Silmarillion, which would eventually be published several years after his death. For once her role in the revolt against the Valar has been established as due to her desire 'to see the wide unguarded lands [of Middle-earth] and to rule there a realm of her own',[29] little else is mentioned of her at all in that book, other than what is discussed above, before she disappears from the story altogether.

Douglas Charles Kane has shown that the way that The Silmarillion was edited from its constituent drafts by Christopher Tolkien diminishes the role of Galadriel as well as omitting other significant female characters. For example,

Galadriel is only described as the most beautiful of all the house of Finwë and not also as the most valiant.[30] From other drafts, however, we know that Galadriel was 'man-high' being six feet four inches in height and that she was 'the greatest of the Noldor, except Fëanor maybe'.[31] Furthermore, The Silmarillion alters the significance of Galadriel's stay in Doriath by suggesting she first met Celeborn there, telling us 'and there was great love between them', when in the source material the 'them' refers to Galadriel and Melian.[32] Most significantly, Kane points out that the published version of The Silmarillion omits several texts that Tolkien was hoping to include as appendices, including two that were subsequently published in Unfinished Tales: 'Concerning Galadriel and Celeborn', an account of their lives in the Second Age, and 'Aldarion and Erendis', a long even-handed story of the uneasy relationship of a king and queen of Númenor that reveals much of Tolkien's rather binary conception of the difference between men and women.[33]

Even more revealing of this binary is 'Atrabeth Finrod Ah Andreth', which concerns Galadriel's brothers Finrod and Aegnor, and the love of the mortal woman Andreth for the latter.[34] This is unique because all the other examples of human-elf relationships in Tolkien involve a mortal man and an immortal elf woman.[35] However, the fact that Andreth's love remains unrequited suggests that Tolkien's belief was that such relationships can only work when the elf chooses to live in the mortal world and by extension that all relationships between men and women can only work on male terms. Finrod tries to persuade an ageing Andreth that the fact that Aegnor did not act on his love for her many years before – 'he withdrew and did not grasp what lay to his hand'[36] – was entirely for her sake. This way she will be relieved of the shame of growing old alongside him, for such marriages can only be for high purposes, brief and hard at the end: 'the least cruel fate that could befall would be that death would soon end it'.[37] A memory that is fair and unfinished is better than one that goes on to a grievous end, Finrod explains, and this way Aegnor will ever remember her 'in the sun of morning'.[38] 'And what shall I remember?' is Andreth's immediate bitter response. Although Tolkien, consciously at least, surely intends his readers to accept Finrod's argument, the emotional impact of the story is generated by Andreth's distress.

Here, as with the story of Arwen, Tolkien's ambivalent attitudes are on display as he demonstrates his awareness that a patriarchal ordering of the world does emotional and symbolic violence to women but nonetheless advocates that women should accept their lot within this system or otherwise be unhappy. This doesn't prevent him from regularly raising the possibility of relationships that transcend such limitations because they begin in versions of Faery. Nevertheless, his commitment to maintain patrilinear hierarchy outweighs his transgressive desires and leads him to represent the 'long defeat' of the Fairy Queen and Faery as inevitable, even as he fetishises the consequent sense of loss. Regardless of whether Galadriel herself would be best served to take the ring from Frodo, I'm tempted to argue that Tolkien might have been able to work through his own conflicting desires better if he had written her as so doing. However, the scene already teeters precariously on the edge of male sexual fantasy. John Boorman and Rospo Pallenberg simply made the latent content manifest when they depicted Galadriel as sexually seducing Frodo in their screenplay, written 1969-70, for a projected film adaptation of The Lord of the Rings.[39]

After spending several months researching, thinking and writing about this question, I've finally concluded that Galadriel actually 'passes the test' by not allowing herself to get caught up in the false binary choice between refusing or accepting the ring. She doesn't have to choose between being the 'White Lady' or the 'Dark Queen' because she is already both of those and all points between. She doesn't have to take the ring to deploy its power. She orchestrates the defeat of Sauron from beginning to end; from first convening the White Council to providing Frodo and Sam with the means – from rope, lembas and elven cloaks to the phial that shines with the light of Eärendil's star – of completing their quest. Most importantly, though, through her 'magical' encounter with Frodo and Sam, which is more of a mutual exchange of power than a seduction scene, she transforms them in ways that Gandalf and Aragorn could not. The immature Sam blushes when Galadriel first looks into his eyes,[40] but later during the most desperate moments in the pass of Cirith Ungol, he is able to transform himself into an elvish warrior after invoking her name.[41] Unlike the discarded human lover of fairy lore, left to pine on the cold hillside, Sam remains infused with the power of Galadriel and Faery.

As Tolkien realised to his own surprise and later came to regret, it is this Sam who becomes the hero of The Lord of the Rings.[42] Not only does he complete the hero's journey by returning home but, when he gets there, he scatters and plants the earth and seeds from Lórien that Galadriel has given him and so effects a magical transformation of the Shire. Within its borders, Sam completes the final stages of his own transformation into a sexual being by marrying Rosie and fathering a daughter named, significantly, after the golden flower of Lórien, Elanor. The implicit promise of a future beyond endless father-son genealogies is held open by the novel's ending, when he sits with Elanor on his lap.[43]

Even though Galadriel is 'robed all in glimmering white' as she, too, returns home at the end of The Lord of the Rings,[44] her smile reminds us that her values are not simply those of the great and the good she has been travelling with. The Fairy Queen remains undefeated. She has passed the 'test' she set herself to simultaneously defeat Sauron and placate the Valar, while using her own power to both change the world and hold open the possibilities of Faery even within an age of men. She didn't have to take the ring because she had the power anyway and she was prepared to use it. There's a lesson there for our own times.

NICK HUBBLE (THEY/THEM) is a writer, editor, reviewer, critic and researcher, who is based in Aberystwyth, Cymru. Nick's work has appeared in Tribune, Jacobin, LA Review of Books, Strange Horizons, ParSec *and* Vector. *They were a judge for the Arthur C. Clarke Award in 2020-21 and 2021-22.*

---

1. J.R.R. Tolkien, *The Fellowship of The Ring*, second edition, London: Allen & Unwin, 1966 [1954], p.281.
2. Tolkien used this spelling in his beautiful late story *Smith of Wootton Major*.
3. Maureen Duffy, *The Erotic World of Faery*, St Albans: Granada, 1974, p.59.
4. See Tom Shippey, *The Road to Middle Earth*, London: Harper Collins, 1992, pp.57-9.

5. See *The Erotic World of Faery*, pp.15-24.
6. *The Erotic World of Faery*, p.93.
7. *Fellowship of the Ring*, p.381.
8. *Fellowship of the Ring*, p.393.
9. J.R.R. Tolkien, *Unfinished Tales*, ed. Christopher Tolkien, London: Unwin Paperbacks, 1982, p.228.
10. *Unfinished Tales*, p.231.
11. *Fellowship of the Ring*, p.287.
12. See *Fellowship of the Ring*, p.81.
13. See J.R.R. Tolkien, *The Treason of Isengard*, ed. Christopher Tolkien, London: Harper Collins, 2015, p. 222.
14. *Treason of Isengard*, p.258.
15. *Treason of Isengard*, p.260.
16. J.R.R. Tolkien, *The Two Towers*, second edition, London: Allen & Unwin, 1966 [1954], p.275.
17. See *Treason of Isengard*, p.448.
18. J.R.R. Tolkien, *The Return of the King*, second edition, London: Allen & Unwin, 1966 [1955], pp.337-44.
19. *Fellowship of the Ring*, p.367.
20. To be precise, the marriage of Aragorn and Arwen reunites the lines of the brothers Elrond and Elros. Arwen is the daughter of Elrond. Aragorn son of Arathorn is the direct father-to-son descendent of Elendil and through Elendil the direct father-to-son descent of Elros. Genealogical tables on pp.347-9 of *The Silmarillion* set out the Noldorin, Sindarin and mortal lines of descent of Elrond and Elros. In this respect, the entire Tolkien legendarium revolves around one bloodline.
21. J.R.R. Tolkien, *The Peoples of Middle Earth*, ed. Christopher Tolkien, London: Harper Collins, 2015, p.185.
22. See J.R.R. Tolkien, *The Silmarillion*, ed. Christopher Tolkien, London: Allen & Unwin, 1977, 30-2, 63.
23. *Silmarillion*, p. 63-4.
24. *Silmarillion*, p. 131.
25. J.R.R. Tolkien, *The War of the Jewels*, ed. Christopher Tolkien, London: Harper Collins, 2015, p.35.
26. See *Fellowship of the Ring*, p.389.
27. J.R.R. Tolkien and Donald Swan, *The Road Goes Ever On: A Song Cycle*, London: Harper Collins, 2002 [1968], p.68.
28. *Fellowship of the Ring*, p.372.
29. *Silmarillion*, p. 96.
30. See Douglas Charles Kane, *Arda Reconstructed: The Creation of the Published Silmarillion*, Bethlehem: Lehigh University Press, 2011,

p.74; *Silmarillion*, p.69; J.R.R. Tolkien, *Morgoth's Ring*, ed. Christopher Tolkien, London: Harper Collins, 2015, p.177.
31. *Unfinished Tales*, pp.229, 286.
32. See *Arda Reconstructed* pp.143-4; *Silmarillion*, p.131; *War of the Jewels*, p.35.
33. See *Arda Reconstructed*, p.250.
34. See *Morgoth's Ring*, pp.303-66. On one of the wrappers of the drafts of this text, Tolkien wrote: '"Should be last item in an index" (i.e. to *The Silmarillion*)', p.329.
35. The other human-elf relationships are: Beren and Lúthien; Tuor and Idril; Eärendil and Elwing (although both are of mixed human-elf heritage, the first is always referred to as a mortal man and the latter as an elf in *The Silmarillion*); Imrazôr the Númenórean and Mithrellas (from whom the Lords of Dol Amroth are descended, see *Unfinished Tales*, p. 248); Aragorn and Arwen.
36. *Morgoth's Ring*, p.324.
37. *Morgoth's Ring*, p.324.
38. *Morgoth's Ring*, p.325.
39. See Nick Groom, *Twenty-First-Century Tolkien*, London: Atlantic Books, 2023, pp.198-208. Boorman's *Excalibur* (1981), which was also scripted with Pallenberg, gives some idea of what their version of *The Lord of the Rings* might have looked like.
40. See *Fellowship of the Ring*, p.372.
41. See *Two Towers*, pp.338-9.
42. See Humphrey Carpenter with Christopher Tolkien, eds, *The Letters of J.R.R. Tolkien*, London: Allen & Unwin, 1981, pp.105, 329. See also Nick Hubble, '"The Choices of Master Samwise": The Literary History of the 1950s' in Nick Bentley, Alice Ferrebe and Nick Hubble, eds, *The 1950s*, London: Bloomsbury, 2018, pp. 22-5.
43. See *Return of the King*, p.311. Tolkien also drafted a closing epilogue that was subsequently not included in the published version of the novel. This featured a conversation between Sam and a teenage Elanor in which he assures her that there will still be great things for her to see and do, and that she too may will face important choices. See J.R.R. Tolkien, *Sauron Defeated*, ed. Christopher Tolkien, London: Harper Collins, 2015, pp. 121-33.
44. *Return of the King*, p.308.

13

FOX GIRL

A SPECULATIVE JOURNEY

LEE MURRAY

 ...three thousand years ago, Foxes were considered wise beings, counselors to the earliest mythical kings of China. They were shapeshifters that could take on human forms both male and female. There were also accounts of Foxes aspiring to enlightenment that would let them transcend their earthly existence. But as Chinese culture became more patriarchal, Fox spirits fell out of favour. They were 'betwixt and between,' not truly human or animal, male or female. They blurred the accepted lines between official and unofficial, private and public, moral and immoral in social and religious practices. By the seventeenth century, Fox spirits had been demoted to creatures that were demonic at worst, unreliable at best. Thus, they were considered suitable for worship only by the most marginalized members of society—women, the poor, sex workers, and actors, the abandoned. (Janie Chang, 2017)

I AM a fox spirit of sorts, although it has only recently been revealed to me in my latest iteration as an Asian diaspora writer of speculative fiction living in the urban wilds of Aotearoa New Zealand.

> *You do not know how you came to be here, a fox spirit in this distant land of dark earth and drifting clouds, a fox spirit so far from the den of the Red Dragon that even the Great Bear has forsaken you, but there is only one way onwards to heaven.* (Lee Murray, 2024, p. 16)

> Since ancient times, foxes have been feared and revered. The very earliest ones, the celestial foxes were regarded as divine beasts. In the Tang and Song dynasties, they acquired a reputation for trickster cunning and the ability to turn themselves into humans. Still, it's mostly peasants who believe in their supernatural powers. (Yangsze Choo, 2024, p. 10)

Without a húli jīng, no village is complete. — Chinese proverb

The fox spirit is a mythological supernatural creature common to many Asian cultures: for example the kitsune in Japan, the kumiho in Korea, and the húli jīng in China. A long-lived creature imbued with cunning and caution, the fox is almost always female and as such is associated with feminine capriciousness and malice. These attributes, coupled with her ability to take on human form, means she can reward or punish the humans she encounters by affecting their wealth, their romantic relationships, and their physical wellbeing. Thus, to ward off the ill-omen that inevitably accompanied the presence of the fox spirit, people would erect household and village shrines to placate and appease her in case she should happen to embody someone they knew. "In Chinese mythology, the fox is a liminal creature," writes my colleague Geneve Flynn in her introduction to my prose-poetry collection *Fox Spirit on a Distant Cloud*. "Untameable and wild, it dwells in the margins and is neither wholly good nor evil. It is a shapeshifter..." (Flynn, 2024, p. 7)

> Shapeshifter. n. one that seems able to change form or identity at will, especially: a mythical figure that can assume different forms (as of animals).

In her novel, *The Fox Wife*, author Yangsze Choo says of the fox spirit that "there are tales of foxes that acquire human form by placing human skulls on their heads and bowing to the moon at midnight. An eerie image, combining all the things that Chinese fear: decay, darkness, moonlight." (Choo, 2024, p. 71) My *Black Cranes* sister, Rena Mason, author of "The Ninth Tale," describes the gruesome process of transformation: "The fox spirit straightened the skullcap, moist with blood, atop her head, then stepped over the decapitated corpse from which she'd taken it." (Mason, 2020, p. 115). In Chinese myth, this ugly act of acquiring and discarding versions of oneself is the fox spirit's only way to enlightenment, as, "according to legend, the húli jīng must endure spiritual cultivation on its path to ascendance and mortality. It tries on skull after skull, taking on different guises, seeing and living the world through many eyes." (Flynn, 2024, p. 10)

The myth of the fox spirit is that she must endure many lives in order ascend to heaven and become divine, in order to achieve immortality. In the course of these lifetimes, she acquires a great deal of knowledge, in itself a source of enlightenment, a means of achieving immortality. The fox spirit has little agency in this, though. She is cursed with living: to survive, she must continually transform and reinvent herself.

> *You must choose one of them. One by one you shall place them on your head, and they shall guide your passage, like stones across a river. Nine slippery steps. Nine spikes on the palace gates.*
> *Nine tails.*
> *Nine tales.*
> *Nine mortal lives.* (Murray, 2024, p. 16)

Throughout my journey to my current form, I have tried on many skulls, some that chafed and constrained, and others that offered a glimpse at my true self. At times, I'll admit that I lost my way, lost sight of myself. "You wonder if there has been some foul perversion or ghostly occurrence that has caused you to lose your way, leaving you placeless, faceless." (Murray, 2024, p. 15) But through these other selves, these skulls I have tried on—some of which I still carry with me—I trace my journey into speculative fiction and my ultimate search for identity and meaning.

Whose Skull is This?

From the moment I was born as the 'half-caste' daughter of a 'white devil' man and a Chinese 'almond-eyed difficulty' of a mother (*West Coast Times*, 1881), I was destined to be a fox spirit. In Aotearoa New Zealand, a country with a history of poll taxes and racist regulations, where a century of Yellow-Peril mistrust of Chinese people still permeated the Kiwi consciousness, and where Chinese European marriages were rare, I immediately became an outsider.

> *When you were born here in the land of the long white cloud, in the savage bushlands of New Zealand; when you were born at the turn of the century, you were a little strangeness, an alien olive strangeness with mysterious almond eyes.* (Murray, 2024, p. 51)

When I started school in a small New Zealand town in 1970, there was no other child who looked like me. Not only did I not see another Asian person in the classroom, I wasn't represented in any of the books I read, the games that we played, or the food that we ate. I wore western clothes and spoke only English. This adherence to the western traditions of my father's family, and of my country's British colonisers, was a conscious decision on the part of my parents. They didn't intend to suppress my Chinese heritage. That wasn't their purpose. Kind and loving, they only wanted the best possible life for me, and for them that meant ensuring I adopted western behaviours. How else would I get ahead? Practically no one spoke my mother's tongue in New Zealand. How would I get a good job? So my mother's languages and her culture were stifled.

The other children weren't fooled. They could tell I didn't belong.

> *You were one-part willow and one-part mānuka, and out-of-place unbelonging strangeness. (Murray, 2024, p. 51)*

There is a danger in being 'other', because "whenever humans encounter something strange and novel, their first instinct is to kill it." (Choo, 2024, p. 64)

The Chinese skull on my head gave me away. My dark hair and almond eyes. Wrists thinner than a sparrow's leg. As Korean American musician, Michelle Zauner, noted in her bestselling book *Crying in H Mart*:

> There was something in my face that the other people deciphered as a thing displaced from its origin, like I was some kind of alien or exotic fruit. "What are you then?' was the last thing I wanted to be asked at twelve because it established that I stuck out, that I was unrecognizable, that I didn't belong. (Zauner, 2021, p. 95)

Far wiser than me, my own child, an unquiet spirit of blended gender and race, says,

> Perhaps the tragedy of the fox demon lies in her inability to land on one form. She is unable

> to fully show herself amongst the hostile eyes of the community, yet she must always carry some aspect of the fox that distinguishes her as an outsider. (Murray, C. 2023, p. 21)

Still, I wore my western mask as much as I could, taking it off only at home. I did not dare to be my true self, my blended whole self, since that life was inherent with risk. Instead, in a strange irony, in trying to become western, I put my head down, lowered my eyes, and became even more typically Chinese—a model minority. My school reports provide the evidence:

Lee is a quiet and studious child.

Lee is polite and well-mannered.

Lee's strengths are in English and language.

> Just as the fox sister must murder to achieve identity, for those who are bi-racial, identity has its own emotional brutality. It comes at a cost. The expunction of one heritage in order to fit into a monoethnic category. (Kristy Kulski, 2023, p. 161)

Thus, from the moment I was born, I was destined to struggle with this brutality.

> Unlike ghosts, [fox spirits] cannot be separated from their body, nor can they flee any physical threats. They can bleed; they can be hunted and killed. Unlike the dead, a fox demon is a creature with her back against the wall. Her

existence depends on her ability to toe the line between the worlds, to appear benign, and without malice. (Murray, C. 2023, p. 19)

the fox hides / among clouds (Murray, 2024, p. 9)

Whose Skull is This?

I grew up in a happy household, full of children and books. My father, the son of a school mistress, taught me to read with flash cards before I went to school. Even before that, when I could barely turn the pages for myself, the family made weekly trips to the local library, coming home with armfuls of books which I devoured. Speculative fiction was my go-to, an escape offering new worlds to inhabit where everyone was other. I read all the sci-fi and fantasy classics on the library shelves, mainly British fare, since New Zealand is part of the commonwealth. Barrie, Tolkien, Lewis, and Carroll were canon of course, and there were newcomers like John Wyndham, Richard Adams, and Alan Garner. Very few titles by women. Even fewer by Chinese writers in translation. When I saw myself represented in a story for the first time, in John Wyndham's 1955 dystopia *The Chryslids*, I would have been in intermediate school.

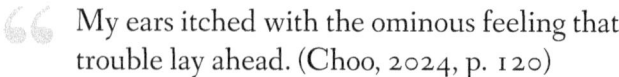 My ears itched with the ominous feeling that trouble lay ahead. (Choo, 2024, p. 120)

In Wyndham's story, the people of post-nuclear Labrador seek redemption for mankind's role in the apocalypse, religiously practising selective eugenics and casting any unpure, undesirable mutants into the wilds of the Fringes.

While hiding from persecution in this hostile environment, mutant teen telepaths learn of a sanctuary, which the author called 'Sealand', after New Zealand. That was the moment the penny dropped. Suddenly, I realised why I was born in this place. Why I was different. I was one of Wyndham's mutants, a monster who'd been whisked across oceans to relative safety in the land of the long white cloud.

> *A bulge appears in those grey cords, pushing and pulsing against your velvet lining. The bulge shifts and grows, shifts and grows, grotesque and expectant, and when you blink a dragon bursts from your body, shearing flesh and spattering blood in your bright-light room.*
>
> *The ghost doctors cannot see it. You're not surprised since they cannot hear either. You are foreign and faraway, and your body is a curio, a curiosity, a difficulty.*
>
> *The dragon, which was just a mouse but has become a monster, bares its golden teeth as it circles the false suns of the ceiling, its whiskers trailing in dark threads that whip around the ghost doctors. It is searching for the sun, for the open air, where it can breathe its dragon-fire and soar in splendid silver dragon waves over the long white cloud to the familiar pink-silk skies.* (Murray, 2024, p. 40).

Yet as my horror sister, Kristy Kulski, author of *The House of Pungsu*, writes in her essay for *Unquiet Spirits*, even home is not safe. "Home became a place where I acutely did not belong. A place where my fiercely New England grandmother would clutch me and proclaim that she would 'knock the slant out' of my eyes." (Kulski, 2023, p. 163)

For the fox spirit, there is always some mutant thing, some vital part that must be cut out of us. And if it cannot be cleaved off, then at the very least, it must be carefully hidden.

> I exist as either a small canid with thick pointed ears, and neat black feet, or a young woman. Neither are safe forms in a world run by men. (Choo, 2024, p. 2)

Whose Skull is This?

> *You are back in the wet leaf litter, beneath the beech trees, near the ancient lake, beside the stinking pile of disembodied skulls.*
> *You have barely started your quest, but already you are bone tired.*
> *Already your marrow chafes with these tiresome tedious lives.* (Murray, 2024, p. 43)

When I was 13, after spending an afternoon reading *Gone with the Wind*, and learning that Margaret Mitchell had been just 25 when she twisted her ankle and started writing the book out of boredom, I announced to my family that I intended to become a writer. A great artist like Mitchell. I was already filling notebooks and school journals with stories and poems, so it made perfect sense. My parents encouraged the notion. As far as they were concerned, there was nothing I couldn't do. But later, when it came time for university, they reminded me of the realities of a life in the arts, of the precariousness of it. They weren't saying I should give up my dream, and they weren't insisting that I get married either, just that I should get a proper job first. They had their reasons. For Chinese families, medicine is the only real profession:

> Like all parents, mine have hopes and dreams for their children. From the beginning, my sisters and I are made clear on some of these dreams. We are all to do well in school. We are all to go to good colleges. We are all to get financially stable jobs. To my parents, being a medical doctor is the best job of all: well-paying, secure, respected by everyone.(Vanessa Fogg, 2023, p. 140)

For my Kiwi dad, whose own father had been a railway guardsman, the move from blue collar hardship to a career in medicine seemed safer. I could always be a writer once I had something behind me to back me up, a hobby for my spare time.

I went to university and promptly failed to be a medical doctor.

My heart wasn't in it.

> A húli jīng was a demon who stole hearts. (Ken Liu, 2016, p. 21)

But since that heart, that skull, were already committed by that point, I pushed on, studying to be a scientist, and also a manager, keeping my passion for literature alive by squeezing in courses on Donne and Joyce in the margins of two graduate degrees. The thing is, scientists and managers are some of the most creative people I know, weaving incredible tales of what if, and why not, and how about, and in that milieu, I gathered ideas for stories, gained critical research skills, and learned something of rigour. And in the process, I accidentally fell in love and married a physicist.

Whose Skull is This?

Fast forward a few years, and we'd lived in four countries and had had two children, one with complex learning needs, and all at once I was wearing three skulls: wife, mother, and daughter. Mostly, I had accepted these skulls, had even wished for them. In the main, they were a good fit. My husband had a good business, but he needed to travel a lot for work. My father was aging, and my mother needed help with his care. The children needed nourishing, with food and stories. I was too busy to write stories. I put aside my dreams of books and tried to be content.

> *Your stomach growls. These lives have left you ravenous.* (Murray, 2024, p. 72)

Finally, when my youngest child started school, my husband declared that it was time for me to stop talking about writing a book and actually write one. The business was doing well enough that we didn't need me to rush back to paid work. We could afford a little time.

While I stammered objections, he slammed the writing skull on my head.

> I had let him do all this to me, to replace me part by part, mourning my loss all the while without understanding what I had gained. A terrible thing had been done to me, but I could also be terrible. (Liu, 2016, p. 32)

So I became a writer. A cursed shapeshifter, who inhabits lives and shapes them to her will.

Whose Skull is This?

I wore the skull, lived the life of a writer, although it was some time before I gave myself permission to call myself a writer. And I rushed in and made a rookie mistake. I chose too safely. I picked up a woman's skull, one that looked like it might fit me comfortably, deciding that I should write women's fiction. I was a woman, after all. So I followed that old adage, writing what I knew, writing what I thought people wanted to read, and penned a romcom about the sweaty awkward path to true love. It was one of those stories where the best friend is the true love who was there all the time. I added workouts at the gym, a local setting in trendy coffee shops, and frosted the narrative with cupcakes. The book was flippant and frivolous and fun, and I learned a lot about writing, about story arcs and character development and theme. Important valuable work. But somehow, that skull left me feeling hollow and unfulfilled.

All at once, I longed to place an ugly skull on my head, a cracked one, festooned with sinew and dripping blood. A haunted skull, where the wind whispered through its orifices with fear and hurt. I realised that I wanted to write about more than cupcakes. I wanted to write about the things that kept me awake at night, the fears I have for the future, for the land that nurtures me, and the people I love. I wanted to share stories from the margins, authentic stories that resonated with my lived experience, and that realisation led me to speculative fiction and horror, because, as Alma Katsu states in her foreword to the anthology *Black Cranes*: "There may not be a more natural paring in all of literature than 'Asian woman' and 'horror'." (Katsu, 2020, p. 11)

> *inside*
> *a man-crafted*
> *box of woman-should*
> *a starving ghost*
>
> *I let her go* ('*fury*' *in* Tortured Willows,
> *p. 32*)

...in the speculative fiction world, I feel it's easier to create a world and control the narrative to write a story that isolates an issue and gives voice to its victims more effectively. In the books I've read by female SF authors, there's more focus on how the imagined society can be made to work or not work, and less on space battles and game-changing technologies. Maybe it's because writers who are 'other' already live in an alternative society of sorts, a between-the-lines subtext kind of existence, where reality often bears little resemblance to the written laws of the land. In fact, you could say that for some writers, a society where they are not marginalized is already the stuff of fantasy. (Chang, 2017)

Whose Skull is This?

Once I discover my love for speculative fiction again, there is no stopping me. I am consumed with it. My work becomes darker and darker. Over the next fifteen years I will write and curate forty books: monster stories, supernatural tales that straddle culture and context, narratives plundered from Aotearoa landscape, stories that speak for the underdog.

Tales where I reveal glimpses of myself. Still a mutant, still monstrous, but no longer completely hidden.

"To be invisible in this world is to have your stories erased or reduced to the margins," wrote Karen Tay in a Stuff article published online in 2020, "which is how it's largely been for many generations of Chinese immigrants to New Zealand. But in the past decade, New Zealand's Chinese diaspora—from Kiwi-born Chinese whose families arrived as long ago as the earliest Pākehā, to recent immigrants—is taking back the power by writing their own stories. They are no longer striving to keep their heads down and completely assimilate. Instead, these writers are sharing their own truths unapologetically and unequivocally... redefining on their own terms, on story at a time: the immigrant narrative."

> *and when at last I slip it on*
> *my tainted blood blooms*
> *red lotuses on sunrise silk*

> *and I smile because it's fitting (from*
> *'cheongsam' in* Tortured Willows, *p. 4)*

Whose Skull is This?

Over time, my speculative writing wins me multiple national and international awards and prizes. A couple of stipends. A residency. An honour from the King. Each accolade adds the burden of another weighty cranium to pinch at my temples.

"Imposter! Imposter!" they clamour as they squeeze ever tighter.

I am always surprised, always sure that there has been some kind of mistake. We foxes are shy creatures, preferring the safety of the shadows. Women too should speak softly and wait to be spoken to. How else have we survived for so long? And yet my writing, unquiet and full of ghosts, has attracted the attention of the gods.

While I am hugely grateful for the acknowledgement, these accolades make me feel like the Roman emperor Commodus, when he fashioned himself as the god Hercules, wearing the head of a lion and carrying a club.

Surely, they will send someone to assassinate me soon.

But as heavy as they are, those skulls have pushed me harder. I have been compelled to work on my writing muscles, strengthening them so that they might bear the weight of those trophies, to prove to myself that I deserved them.

There is another reward. While I have been writing my monster stories, setting them in Aotearoa and filling them with women who look like me, I have somehow gathered powerful communities about me. It is the rarest thing. Foxes are usually solitary beings, and yet they have found me. Among the most important to me is my connection to other Asian women writing horror and speculative stories, contributors to my anthologies and supporters of my work. The groundswell began with my *Black Cranes* sisters, then *Tortured Willows*, and even more *Unquiet Spirits*... Perhaps global events have had something to do with it, or perhaps it might have happened anyway, but suddenly I am at the nucleus of Asian diaspora horror narratives, a fledging subgenre still wet with blood.

 ...she began to notice the presence of foxes. One by one, they appeared in the fog, yowling and moaning in unison with the bell. From the verdant green hills, they walked toward her. Must have been hundreds of them, immigrant foxes, their tails curled over their bodies—some had one tail, some had seven, some had four. In the human-made thunder of the bells, Mindy waited for hers to arrive.(Sally Wen Mao, 2024, p. 194)

So now I keep company with foxes. These fox-women buoy me up and give me courage. Despite the subversive and transgressive nature of our genre, they remind me that our stories have value, not for the awards and the prizes, but for the connection they represent.

Whose Skull is This?

 Imagine you are a young woman. Imagine you want to cry, but you can't because of a sickness where your eyes make flies instead of tears. You've had this illness since the first day you turned into an adult, but you don't remember that day because you don't remember a day in your life when it was okay for you to cry. Every time you cry flies come out of your eyes, and they are loud and brash with the freshness of being alive and they destroy everything: subway rides, dinner parties, family outings, relationships, silence, you name it. (Wen Mao, 2024, p. 165)

In Lela Lee's graphic novel *Angry Little Asian Girl: Moments with my Mother*, there is a comic strip that comprises two characters: a mental health therapist, and an Asian girl named Kim. In an image that resembles the classic Shulz/Peanuts' "the doctor is in" strip, Kim arrives at her mental health service appointment wearing a hat and glasses. The text reads:

 Kim: Hi.

Therapist: Hi Kim. Why the disguise?

Kim: My mom told me Asians don't go to therapy because we'll lose 'face'.

Therapist: ?

Kim: So I put on an extra face just in case.

Like Kim's Korean heritage, my Chinese heritage demands that mental illness be denied, or hidden behind a mask, which serves to exacerbate the crippling stigma, contributing further to the loneliness and alienation experienced by sufferers. My European heritage also prefers to sequester away such unpleasantness, lest the malady be catching. Better to hide the offensive person in an attic or keep them straitjacketed in an asylum, than have the monster rampage through society causing harm, at least if a host of 70s horror movies are to be believed. And yet when it comes to mental illness, revealing something of our lived experience, even the monstrous parts, can not only be cathartic, but can offer a chance for shared connection, understanding and solace. "Sometimes, showing a little of ourselves, then more over time, makes them fear us less." (Mason, 2020, p. 127)

> She wasn't exactly a friend. More like someone you couldn't help being drawn to because you shared knowledge of how the world didn't work the way you had been told. (Liu, 2016, p. 25)

I was not diagnosed with anxiety and depression—with flies in my eyes as Sally Wen Mao describes it—until I reached my 50s, and as a result a more recent iteration of my writing life has been as an advocate for the positive portrayal of mental illness in speculative and horror narratives, for example as co-founder of the Horror Writers Association's Wellness Committee, and more recently as co-editor (with Dave Jeffery) of Flame Tree Press's forthcoming anthology *This Way Lies Madness*. This skull is still raw and occasionally hard to wear, yet I am especially proud of it. It's one I hope to wear for a while yet.

> The way we live, always on the edge, running along the tops of stone walls and fences. Between civilisation and the wilderness. (Choo, 2024, p. 49)

Whose Skull is This?

> Throughout her life, Kuzuha had always had the feeling that she was just pretending to be a regular woman. Of course, that was the path she had selected as a shortcut, and she had never once doubted that her decision had been the right one. But one day as she studied her aging face in the mirror, a face whose eyes seemed more vulpine than ever, a face that the years had made even narrower, it occurred to Kuzuha that she really was a fox—a fox who had totally forgotten that she had transformed into a person at some point along the line. (Aoko Matsuda, 2016, p. 140)

My journey to become a speculative writer has been one of many decades. All these skulls. These lives. Still, I am unsure if I have found my true place. Even now I cannot be certain I am telling the right story. All I can do is select the next skull and place it on my head in the hope that it shall guide my passage, another stepping stone in the river towards something higher.

From animal to a complete human being.

"The whole idea of 'are you human?' speaks to a very ancient kind of reaction to a stranger," Yangsze Choo says in a February 2024 interview about *The Fox Wife*, published in *The Straits Times*: "You try to judge if a person is trustworthy. It is a means of trying to put all the strangeness into a box, so that you can react."

> The story usually ends with the shapeshifting fox boiled to death or skewered by an angry mob. That shouldn't happen, however, if you're careful. Most foxes are. How else could we survive for hundreds of years? (Choo, 2024, p. 2)

Is it enough to not be boiled to death? Foxes long to be our true selves, to shout our stories from the rooftops, so we might be heard and understood.

> I dream of my true form leaping from beam to ledge to terrace to roof, until I am at the top of this island, until I can growl in the faces of all the men who believe they can own me. (Liu, 2016, p. 29)

In his fox spirit story, "Good Hunting", Liu claims that in the meantime "there is only one thing we can do: Learn to survive." (Liu, 2016, p. 26) That seems like sound advice. After all, "if you can survive for a thousand years, you may reach enlightenment. Or so they say." (Choo, 2024, p. 224)

Or so they say…

References

Chang, J. (2017). Ghosts and Fox Spirits: Janie Chang on the Power of Speculative Fiction. *Room Magazine.* Retrieved from https://roommagazine.com/whats-new/interview/ghosts-and-fox-spirits-janie-chang-on-the-power-of-speculative-fiction-2/

Choo, Y. (2024). *The Fox Wife*. Quercus Editions, London.

Choo, Y. (2024) Malaysian author Choo Yangsze on the complex symbolism of fox spirits. *The Staits Times.* 24 February 2024. Retrieved from https://www.straitstimes.com/life/arts/malaysian-author-choo-yangsze-on-the-complex-symbolism-of-fox-spirits

Flynn, G. (2024). "Foreword". *Fox Spirit on a Distant Cloud* by Lee Murray. The Cuba Press, Wellington. pp. 7-10.

Fogg, V. (2023). "Hungry Ghosts in America". *Unquiet Spirits: Essays by Asian Women in Horror* edited by Lee Murray & Angela Yuriko Smith. Black Spot Books, USA. pp. 139-153.

Katsu. A. (2020). *Black Cranes: Tales of Unquiet Women* edited by Lee Murray & Geneve Flynn. Omnium Gatherum. pp. 11-14

Kulski, K. P. (2023). "100 Livers". *Unquiet Spirits: Essays by Asian Women in Horror* edited by Lee Murray & Angela Yuriko Smith. Black Spot Books, USA. pp. 157-166.

Lee, L. (2022). *Angry Little Asian Girl: Moments With my Mother*. Angry Little Girls Inc.

Liu, K. "Good Hunting." *Asian Monsters* edited by Margrét Helgadóttir. Fox Spirit Books, UK. pp. 21-34.

Mason, R. (2020). "The Ninth Tale". *Black Cranes: Tales of Unquiet Women* edited by Lee Murray & Geneve Flynn. Omnium Gatherum. pp. 115-128.

Matsuda, A. (2016). *Where the Wild Ladies Are* translated by Polly Barton. Soft Skull. New York.

Murray, C. (2023). "Fox Daughter". *Unquiet Spirits: Essays by Asian Women in Horror* edited by Lee Murray & Angela Yuriko Smith. Black Spot Books, USA. pp. 17-23.

Murray, L. (2024) *Fox Spirit on a Distant Cloud*. The Cuba Press, Wellington.

Murray, L. (2021). Excerpts from poems in *Tortured Willows: Bent, Bowed, Unbroken* by Christina Sng, Angela Yuriko Smith, Lee Murray & Geneve Flynn. Yuriko Publishing, USA.

Tay, K. (2020). Time for Chinese New Zealanders to be Heard. *Stuff.* 10 May 2020. Retrieved from https://www.stuff.co.nz/entertainment/books/121343588/time-for-chinese-new-zealanders-to-be-heard

Wen Mao, S. (2024). *Nine Tales*. Penguin Books.

West Coast Times, Issue 3703, 16 February 1881, p. 2 Retrieved from https://paperspast.natlib.govt.nz/newspapers/WCT18810216.2.7

Zauner, M. (2021). *Crying in H Mart*. Alfred A. Knopf.

. . .

LEE MURRAY ONZM IS A WRITER, editor, poet and screenwriter from Aotearoa New Zealand, a Shirley Jackson Award and five-time Bram Stoker Award® winner. A USA Today bestselling author with more than forty titles to her credit, including novels, collections, anthologies, nonfiction, poetry, and several books for children, she holds a New Zealand Prime Minister's Award for Literary Achievement in Fiction, the first author of Asian descent to achieve this, and is an Honorary Literary Fellow of the New Zealand Society of Authors. Her latest work, NZSA Cuba Press Prize-winner Fox Spirit on a Distant Cloud, was released in 2024 from The Cuba Press. Lee is the current co-chair (with Dave Jeffery) of the Horror Writers Association Wellness Committee. Read more at leemurray.info

www.speculativeinsight.com

Subscribe for access to all 24 essays throughout the year, and the six-monthly ebooks collecting those essays plus bonus pieces.

www.ingramcontent.com/pod-product-compliance
Lightning Source LLC
Chambersburg PA
CBHW061207070526
44583CB00025B/3153